with all best wishes

Doris.

GW00724656

REFLECTIONS
FROM A
SNOWHOUSE

REFLECTIONS FROM A SNOWHOUSE

F.W. Peacock
with
Lawrence Jackson

Jesperson Press

ST. JOHN'S, NEWFOUNDLAND

Jesperson Press
26A Flavin Street
St. John's, Newfoundland

Text and Cover Design: Alan J. de Gonzague
Cover Illustration: Al Viscount
Illustrations: Doris Peacock
Typesetting: Jesperson Press
Printing & Binding: Jesperson Printing Ltd.

Appreciation is expressed to The Canada Council for its assistance in publishing this book.

The publisher acknowledges the financial contribution of the Cultural Affairs Division of the Department of Culture, Recreation and Youth, Government of Newfoundland and Labrador which has helped make this publication possible.

Canadian Cataloguing in Publication Data

Peacock, F.W. (Frederick William), 1907-1985.
  Reflections from a snowhouse

Includes index.
ISBN 0-920502-72-5

1. Peacock, F.W. (Frederick William), 1907-1985.
2. Missionaries—Newfoundland—Labrador—Biography.
3. Moravian Church—Newfoundland—Labrador—Clergy—
Biography. 4. Moravian Church—Missions—
Newfoundland—Labrador—History.
I. Jackson, Lawrence, 1942-   II. Title.

BX8593.P43A3 1986   266'.467182'0924   C86-093737-2

Dedicated to all those who have been a part of our lives and have by their love and friendship contributed to our happiness, in the hope that we, in some small way, have added to theirs.

ACKNOWLEDGEMENTS

I gratefully acknowledge the assistance of the Canada Council, the help of Dick Buehler of Memorial University, and the help and encouragement of my wife, Doris.

F.W. Peacock

PREFACE

The first time I met the Rev. F. W. Peacock I was still a medical student working with my father on the hospital ship *Maraval* during the summer holidays. As soon as the anchor was down Bill came aboard to greet us and offer any help he could. Although he was not much older than myself and only in his second year as a Moravian Missionary, he was already assuming considerable responsibility — which he describes rather modestly in this book — and was busily learning the Inuit language.

A gracious and friendly young man, he did everything possible to help us in our clinics, including interpreting for the Inuit. He was fast learning this very intricate language. In fact he was to spend a fair part of his life interpreting in Labrador, and later in St. John's, and many people will remember his patience and kindness in undertaking this service for all who needed his help and knowledge.

It is not surprising that he became one of the world's authorities on Inuktitut, the Inuit language, and he has, of course, left us his excellent dictionaries, grammars and other works which have done much to help preserve this difficult tongue. They represent a vast amount of scholarship and labour.

Bill, and later his wife Doris, were both remarkably well equipped for the life work they undertook, and their efforts to preserve as much as possible of the Inuit culture have been of immense value. He was uniquely qualified to do this — the right man at the right time, for

Labrador was about to 'open up' and would soon be deluged with a host of outsiders including the builders and staff of military establishments, civil servants, teachers, researchers, business men and many others.

He was appointed Superintendent of the Moravian Missions for Labrador in 1941 and provided wise and far-sighted leadership for his people, encouraging them to retain as much as possible of the Labrador way of life and to manage their own affairs. His advice was much respected by settlers and Inuit alike.

It is Bill, the man, that I remember best and with great affection. His sense of fun, his warmth, his all-encompassing kindness to his neighbours, visitors and guests—of whom he had a great many—endeared him to us all. Bill had a good practical knowledge of basic medicine and first aid and did much to ease pain and to heal, and his judgement was very sound. He was consultant on every imaginable subject, from the problems of his parishioners to advice for the lovelorn, comfort for those in need, help for those in trouble with authority of any kind, and much else, and he always found some way to help. He never turned anyone away.

He was the best kind of minister, with a gentle but positive attitude and understanding, and he personally exemplified his own beliefs. One never left his church without feeling better, and his sermons were very appropriate for both Inuit and settler. Certainly he affected innumerable lives in the north.

He provided wise leadership, he built well and strongly, and he always championed the Inuit and encouraged them to take pride in their past and to remember who they were.

Personally I think I remember him best and most often from the days we travelled together by dogteam, by boat or by bush airplane. His sense of humour overcame any delays, frustrations, or indeed hardships, and he was wonderfully good company with an agile and far-ranging mind. Hard travelling conditions, bad flying weather and resultant delays never seemed to bother him greatly, he was quite happy in a snowhouse or a tent or aboard a ship, or in some isolated home along the trail, and he was welcomed wherever he went.

This book is a cheerful one, and modestly written, but it is a unique source of information about the Northern people and their way of life and his affection for them is manifest throughout.

Lieutenant-Governor Anthony Paddon
May 7, 1986

FOREWORD

Looking back over thirty-six years among the Inuit and settlers of northern Labrador, I realize how much we all owe each other. Our lives have been interlocked like the pieces of a jigsaw puzzle.

If my wife, Doris, and I have any regrets it is that our hopes and plans for our Labrador friends were not always achieved, because we sometimes lacked the skills we needed for our work and the wisdom to look far enough ahead. I hope that history will be tolerant of our mistakes and that our Inuit and settler brethren and sisters will know that we always tried to act with love, understanding and forbearance.

F. W. Peacock

REFLECTIONS
FROM A
SNOWHOUSE

I had been lying awake for some time, disturbed by the snoring of our two Inuit drivers, and was finally drifting into sleep when my companion yanked me back to reality.

"Bill!" His voice was urgent. "Bill, I've got lice. In fact, I'm lousy."

"What do you expect me to do about it? Put out some traps and be quiet."

I pulled the flaps of my sleeping bag over my head and tried to slip back into sleep. The snoring continued, and in a few minutes my lousy companion had joined the chorus. But now I was wide awake, my mind poring over the events of the day.

From early dawn on that May morning we had travelled by dog sled from Nutak, some forty miles north of Nain. It was a wearying journey across the sea ice past Udlik and Tasiuyak Bay, then along the steep gully of Korokuluk Brook into the heart of the Kiglapait Mountains. Our progress had been painfully slow, especially along the brook, where deep snow required the use of snowshoes. Towards dusk our drivers had suggested we call it a day. So there on the edge of a lake high in the Kiglapaits they quickly found the right snow and built us a snowhouse.

I was given my usual task, packing loose snow into the cracks between the drifted snow blocks of our shelter. My companion, the doctor, lit the primus stove while the drivers unharnessed the dogs, unloaded the sleds and brought everything we needed inside. Before I had finished chinking the gaps, one Inuk had hurried off with the kettle and returned with water for our tea. I couldn't imagine he found it so quickly. When the chores were finished we were glad to be inside, drinking tea and eating hard bread and baked beans. Our dogs, curled up outside, went unfed.

As soon as we had eaten we crawled into our sleeping bags, smoked our pipes and talked awhile before blowing out the candles. The two Inuit were quickly asleep, and I had almost joined them when the doctor roused me with his complaint about the lice.

Now I was facing not only my wakefulness but my doubts. I reflected on why I had come to Labrador, how I was coping with the demands of missionary life, and whether it was worth it.

As a teenager in Bristol, England, I had felt that I must devote my life to spreading the Christian faith; I was possessed with the vision of One who was able to free men from their fears. Because of the compassion I saw in my own father's life, I came to share his concern for the underprivileged. I believed that the Gospel of Jesus Christ demanded social action, and I was determined that if it were in my power I would make some effort to improve the lot of poor people living overseas.

So here I was. There was so much to be done, so much to ponder that my mind was in turmoil, but at last the weary body took over and I slipped into a dreamless sleep.

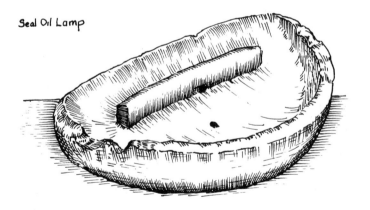

Seal Oil Lamp

1

SETTING OUT

I had not always been a member of the Moravian Church. I was born a Methodist and had hoped to train as a missionary in that denomination. Twice I had stumbled at the final hurdle: interviews with the admission authority of theological schools. At the United Methodist College in Manchester, England, I was far too ready to dispute the notions of the examining board and to put forth my own. So my hopes of entering theological college were temporarily stalled. I was not excited by the suggestion that I train for a more subordinate position where, presumably, I might learn my place.

I applied to an Anglican institution, the Bible Churchman's College. Not being Anglican was the least of my troubles here. The chief difficulty came when I admitted in my interview that I did not believe that the Holy Bible is the infallible word of God. This clearly made me unacceptable. However, the principal advised, if I were able to return in six months and acknowledge my error, I might then be admitted. This, of course, I was not prepared to do.

Then I discovered the Moravians. I began to attend the Moravian Church near my home in Bristol, and found in the services of the Brethren a simple dignity unblemished by ostentation, repetition or long, rambling sermons and prayers. I began to read as much as I could about their history and their record of missionary endeavour. With their emphasis on the Headship of Christ, ecumenism and missionary service, their sense of brotherhood and dedication, they appealed to my own feelings about Christianity. I had found my spiritual home.

I learned that the Moravians had sent out their first missionaries to St. Thomas in the West Indies in 1732, and to Greenland the year after. Twenty years later, after active missionary effort in many parts of the world, they made their first attempt to evangelize the Inuit of Labrador. This ended in failure and tragedy with the death of the expedition leader, his aide, the ship's captain and four sailors, all apparently murdered by the Inuit.

In 1771, they tried again. Jens Haven, a former Greenland missionary, set up a mission station at Nunaingok, afterward named Nain, in northern Labrador. The story of the next two hundred years is one of expansion and retreat, success and failure, dedication and courage, as missions were established along the entire north coast from Killinek, at the northern tip of Labrador, to Happy Valley at the head of Lake Melville.

In September of 1935 I had, as yet, no idea that I would soon become part of this story. I was twenty-eight and a student in the Moravian Theological College in Fairfield, Manchester, preparing to attend a student conference in Switzerland before entering my final year. I was looking forward to an easy year, with only two courses left to complete.

Then out of the blue came a telegram from the Moravian Mission Board in London. An emergency had arisen in Labrador; would I serve there? I had been hoping to be sent to a mission in Tibet, but in those days one accepted a call wherever it led. A quick visit to mission headquarters and an equally speedy interview with the board confirmed the arrangements. I was to sail from Liverpool in three weeks on the S. S. *Newfoundland* of the Furness–Withy Line. If I reached St. John's after the last regular steamer had left for Labrador, I should make my own arrangements to get to Hopedale. This was alarming news for a traveller who had never been outside England.

I would be ordained a deacon on the 22 September, two days before I sailed. In the meantime I could proceed with my plans to attend the conference in Switzerland. Off I went to Basle, leaving my sisters and my fiancée, Doris, to buy my outfit.

While I was gone my mother, doubtless alarmed by the little she knew of Labrador, found in an army surplus store a pair of heavy, rough, grey flannel pyjamas. When the time came to use them I found them warm but maddeningly rough; they languished in a drawer for seven years until my resourceful wife recycled them, tailoring an excellent summer suit. I wore it with pride for years and enjoyed boasting, "Yes, it was tailored for me right here in Labrador."

I returned from Switzerland with barely a week to get ready. I was ordained by the Right Reverend Zippel in Kingswood, Bristol, and set out two days later. My invalid mother, who had never travelled far from her native Bristol, refused to let me leave England without someone waving goodbye, so she joined me on the train to Liverpool. This expedition would have been impossible without my brother-in-law, Len Sexton, who now took my place as the head of the family. (Father had died in 1932 at the age of forty-nine.) Len and my sister, Grace, were exceedingly kind to Doris during the years of our separation. Len was an idealist who became the secretary of a trade union, a job which finally killed him.

The first day out from Liverpool, the sea was deceitfully calm. I felt fine, joining other passengers in deck games. The following morning I went cheerfully off to breakfast, but had to give it up after only a few bites. I returned to the dining hall a second and third time, working on the theory that if I really must be sick it would be wise to have something to be sick with. Each time I had to retreat.

During the morning I became increasingly wretched. I feared that I might die before I reached Newfoundland, and that I might not. When the dulcimer called the hardy to lunch I staggered into the dining room and repeated the morning's performance. I reeled back to my cabin and fell exhausted into my bunk. I dragged myself to afternoon tea with the same result. At dinner that evening my condition was the subject of bets. Staggering back to my cabin, I devoutly wished to die while I still had part of my stomach left.

As the evening progressed, I began to recover. Indeed, before retiring I ate a hearty meal of sandwiches. During the night, I finished most of a large dish of fruit which a thoughtful steward had placed beside my bed. I have occasionally suffered seasickness since, but never the misery of my second day out on the restless Atlantic.

Standing on the deck as we steamed through the Narrows into St. John's harbour, on 30th September 1935, I heard for the first time the "Ode to Newfoundland," sung by a small group of homecoming Newfoundlanders. Whenever I hear that song I still remember my thrill and apprehension that day, gliding between those rocky cliffs, skirting the fishing stages, flakes and weathered timber houses which clung precariously to the rock.

My apprehensions were soon swept aside by the amazing hospitality of Newfoundlanders. The first was a representative of Job Brothers, the Mission agent in St. John's, who had reserved accommodations for me in the old Balsam Hotel, in Barnes Place. Here I was treated very kindly. However, the friendliness of everyone I met during those fifteen days in St. John's was somewhat chilled by their warning of the terrors of winter in Labrador. One morning I met an old woman on the hotel stairway who asked, "Are you the young man who is going to live down on the Labrador among the Eskimos?" When I confirmed this she shook her head sadly and murmured, "Oh, you poor, poor boy." The look of pity on her face was almost too much for me.

During the next two weeks I heard more and more about the inhospitable coast of Labrador. I got plenty of advice, much of it meaningless until I reached that barren coast and could put it in context.

In the meantime, I found a great deal to interest me in St. John's, chiefly because of its association with my home town of Bristol. My early years had been spent beneath the shadow of the Cabot Tower, named for the British discoverer of Newfoundland. At the Bristol Art Gallery, the huge painting of John Cabot setting out from Bristol in his ship the *Matthew* was a strong childhood memory. The King's reward of twelve pounds "to hym that found the new isle," was paid by a Richard Amerycke, collector of customs. There are some who believe that America was named for this man rather than Amerigo Vespucci, as is commonly taught. It is true that Vespucci was a friend of Columbus, but Amerycke was a more prominent man in his day. Moreover, it was not the custom to use Christian names in the naming of newly-discovered lands, unless the name was preceded by some title.

The night before I left St. John's on the last leg of my voyage to Labrador, I had a party in my honour in the home of the late Joseph Keough, an employee of Job Brothers. Nothing was too much trouble for this family. They helped me to fall in love with Newfoundland and they, with others, did much to combat the loneliness I had felt on my arrival. They have remained my lifelong friends.

Late on the evening of 13 October I boarded the S.S. *Kyle*, making a late, unscheduled trip as far as Hebron, in northern Labrador. Passengers, friends and onlookers swarmed over the ship, for in those days the departure of the *Kyle* was an event of some importance. On board were a dozen or more of the newly-formed Newfoundland Rangers, whose posting in remote villages was in fact the reason for this late voyage. Down in the cargo was the lumber for their houses, which they were expected to build before winter.

The Keoughs, of course, saw me off. I felt I was leaving family behind as the *Kyle* pulled out of the railway dock at midnight. A chorus of "Auld Lang Syne" rang from the dock and the vessel. It was a moving occasion mingled with sadness and hope, for here I was on the last leg of the journey which was to take me to my life's work, leaving behind me everything I knew. I was expected to work for seven years before I could take a furlough.

The journey along the northeast coast of Newfoundland and the coast of Labrador seemed hazardous and difficult, beset by wind, rain, fog and blizzard. At one point the decks of the *Kyle* were covered by many inches of snow. Although I have taken that same voyage many times since, I have not lost my respect for the captains of the steamers and schooners which sailed these dangerous waters without the instruments most vessels carry today. Captain Connors, skipper of the *Kyle*, was only the first to arouse my admiration for his handling of our ship along that fierce, rocky, island-studded coast.

Our voyage was enlivened by the presence of the Newfoundland Rangers. Among them was one who became a lifelong friend, Corporal Frank Mercer, later a staff sergeant in the Royal Canadian Mounted Police. Many years later I had the honour of pinning his thirty-year service medal on him. Frank had a sense of humour surpassed, in those days, only by his appetite. I recall one meal during the voyage when he finished a third bowl of soup and asked for more. The steward took an oversized tureen from the sideboard, filled it with soup and solemnly placed it before Frank, who then finished it. With the soup course out of the way, the steward asked if he would like roast beef, roast pork or corned beef. "That will do," said Frank, and ate all three, with vegetables.

The journey along the Labrador coast is always fascinating, with scores of tiny summer fishing settlements set in the most unlikely places, in barren, windy sites chosen almost solely on the basis of their access to fish, with little regard for comfort or shelter. By the time of our trip, however, most people had retreated to their winter communities in the deeper bays and inlets. Time after time our vessel would anchor in a small cove with a handful of houses clinging to the shore. Wherever there was freight to be unloaded, our siren would shriek the announcement of our arrival. The clanking of our donkey engine would be followed by the howling of dogs on shore, then by the putt-putt of the single-stroke, make-and-break engines of the open trap boats in which residents slowly chugged their way to our side.

Sometimes the ship would slide into bays in which there was not the slightest sign of life or habitation, but no sooner was the anchor dropped than we heard the sound of these single-cylinder engines. Soon, trap boats would appear around some rocky headland farther in the bay.

I don't know how many times we dropped anchor or hove to after we left St. Anthony on the northern tip of Newfoundland, but at every place the land disgorged its bevy of boats. They brought to our gangway weatherbeaten folk in windbreakers, parkas and guernseys. Some of the faces had Eskimo features; nearly all had the stamp of hardship and many showed great character, a granite-like quality which adversity had marked but not subdued.

I met my first full-blooded Inuk at Rigolet, near the mouth of Hamilton Inlet. Here, the older men were proud of their racial heritage but the younger men seemed to have no interest in their past or in Inuktut, their language. The situation remains very much the same today, except that the indifferent young men I met forty-five years ago are now among those who cling fiercely to the language, while today's youth are still indifferent.

In 1935 the most southerly of the Moravian stations was at Makkovik. It was here that I first stepped ashore in Labrador, my new home. I was met aboard ship by the Reverend George W. Sach, who had recently taken charge of the Makkovik station. I was to fill the position he had just left, as assistant to the missionary at Hopedale. Joining Reverend Sach I clambered very cautiously down the gangway into an open boat and went ashore to visit his house and family.

Here I learned, to my shock, that when I reached Hopedale I would be responsible for the routine medical work in that district. A doctor from the International Grenfell Association visited the missions once, and sometimes twice, each year. Between these visits medical care of residents fell to mission staff, most of whom had at least some training. I did not.

In the motor boat which took me back to the *Kyle* about midnight, I was joined by a Scot, a fellow passenger making a round trip on the *Kyle*, buying fur. A former Hudson's Bay Company factor, he had been celebrating with old friends at the company house in Makkóvik, and he was drunk. Our boatmen had to wrestle him up the gangway. With this accomplished, they set out again for shore and left me alone on deck with the Scot, who suddenly decided he wished to return as well and tried to climb the rail, apparently intending to swim. It was only with great difficulty that I restrained him and wheedled him into descending the companionway to his cabin.

Here he began in a very loud voice to criticize the Grenfell Mission and two of its doctors, who were aboard as passengers taking a young Makkovik girl back to Cartwright for an appendix operation. (The *Kyle* would not call here again on its return from Nain, so the girl had to make the long detour north to Nain before she could reach the nursing station in Cartwright.) The two doctors were Harry Paddon and a young woman, both of whom had boarded the ship at Cartwright and were *en route* to England on furlough. My noisy companion proclaimed that to take a young child away from home so late in the shipping season was criminal; she would be stranded far from her family until the following summer. The doctors should perform surgery here on board, or in Makkovik.

All this commotion aroused the occupants of the neighbouring cabin, and out stepped Dr. Harry Paddon. The drunk demanded to see his credentials and loudly questioned his competence. Eventually we managed to get him into his cabin and into bed.

So began my friendship with the remarkable Dr. Paddon, which lasted until his death only five years later. He was quiet, competent, utterly dedicated and rather given to understatement, especially in reference to his own work. I have always felt that he did more for the people of Labrador, and of southern Labrador especially, than the famous head of the mission, Sir Wilfred Grenfell. Blessed with great humour and a love of man and Christ, Dr. Paddon went about his work with quiet efficiency. His dog team drivers had great admiration for his ability and endurance in winter travel. Hour after hour he would run beside the *komatik*, or sled, and help the driver clear tangled dogs' traces or ice the runners. He was a welcome guest in every house on the coast.

After his death, his wife carried on his work with the same devotion until their son Anthony, known to us as Tony, who had served as a doctor in the Royal Canadian Navy during the war, took up his father's work. Tony continued in the family tradition, devoting his skills to the people of Labrador. His life and mine have touched at many points over the last fifty years; we travelled many times by boat, dog team or plane together, though he always claimed a reluctance to travel with me, for I developed a reputation as a jinx for weather.

I should not close this chapter without acknowledging that the Scot did me a further service besides provoking my acquaintance with Harry Paddon. Before we settled him in his cabin he insisted on selling me his caribou skin *kollitak*, or parka. I could not resist; the price was right and the garment was not only beautiful but immensely practical, though I could scarcely be sure of this at the time. As I found in the next few winters, there are few things so light and warm as caribou skin with its hollow hair. The Scot assured me, quite truthfully as it turned out, that I could not buy such a garment in Hopedale.

2

HOPEDALE

On the fifteenth day of our passage from St. John's, I awoke early despite my late-night struggle with the drunken fur buyer. We were nearing Hopedale, my destination in a voyage which had begun almost five weeks before. My heart sank a little as we came in sight of the village. The vast mission house and its church dominated the foreground, overshadowing the poor, rather shabby houses of the village. Behind them was a small woodland, and looming over the whole scene was a high, forbidding hill. The village seemed to occupy a rocky mound thrust out into the ocean.

My spirits rose with the approach of a small flotilla of open boats crowded with short, dark-eyed men and women. One of the boats brought a group of men with brass instruments, who struck up "From Greenland's Icy Mountains," followed by the doxology, "Now Thank We All Our God," as they approached the *Kyle*. Soon they were clambering all over the ship. Many came up and shyly took my hand, saying *Aksunai*, which I had already learned was the Inuit greeting, "Be strong." It seemed fitting.

A few minutes later a big man with a ruddy complexion and a heavy grey moustache greeted me heartily. This was the Reverend Walter Whatley Perrett, an Englishman who had served the Mission in Labrador for forty-five years. Pa Perrett was to be my mentor and boss for the following year and my friend to the end of his life. It was through his help that I began my study of the Inuit language, for he was himself a great Inuktut scholar.

I had already met one daughter, Alice, a teacher in Makkovik. Now I was to meet two more and also Mrs. Perrett, a bright-eyed little lady with some odd mannerisms. Ma Perrett mothered, I could almost say smothered me over the next several months, to the point of reporting me to the superintendent of the Mission for not wearing enough clothes. Her idea of adequate clothing was long johns in the heat of summer. Her other two daughters were Edna, the postmistress in Hopedale, and Gladys, who was bedridden and needed much attention.

I was shown to my quarters, a sitting room and bedroom on the second floor, at the west end of the mission house. As in Makkovik, the living quarters here were heated by tall, glazed tile Dutch stoves which burned wood and coal. They were of excellent design, and most efficient.

Hopedale

The Mission no longer needed all of this huge building, which included a carpenter's shop and a smithy in addition to the living quarters. The lower floor was leased to the Hudson's Bay Company for housing its staff. This arrangement was an inconvenience to both groups, particularly during parties held by the lively young men who conducted the company's business.

We had come ashore just in time for the noon meal. Here for the first time I encountered seal meat. I have always been a little finicky about food and wondered if I could adapt to the diet of this strange land. This dark meat did little to reassure me at first glance. However, it was excellently cooked and while I cannot say I enjoyed it, I found it edible and ate a hearty meal.

I was anxious to unpack, to make my sparse quarters a little more homey. Mr. Perrett told me to take my time at this but to let him know when I was done, as he had a job for me. When the time came, he led me outdoors to the back of the house and passed me a long pole, at the end of which was nailed a fourteen pound butter tin. This was ominous. It grew more so when he led me to the cess pit which served the mission's two toilets. We ladled its contents into a barrel, luckily fitted with handles at each side, and lugged it to a dumping spot where voracious huskies immediately gulped its contents. One of the dogs fell in and I was obliged to save its miserable life by hauling it out.

When this vile task was finally done, the old gentleman looked me up and down with twinkling eyes and pronounced, "You'll do." He added, "The next time you can get someone from the village to help you."

I returned to the house for a bath, in a tub filled from boilers on the wood stove. As I soaked I reflected on the limitations of theological school, which had not braced me for chores like this. Later, while on furlough in England, I was invited to address the sanitation officers of the City and County of Bristol on the subject of sanitation in northern Labrador. In spite of my introduction to cess pits and scavenging dogs I declined, wondering what I could say, beyond "practically none."

Having measured me with this task, Pa Perrett proceeded to father and guide me in all that I did. I would begin teaching school the following morning, joining Edna and her mother at classes held in the Mission house. I would begin my study of Inuktut right after supper. Pa handed me a pile of school exercise books and said, "This is the Eskimo grammar, the only copy in English. You will need to copy it." (When I finally completed this task , it covered 260 foolscap pages in my very tiny writing.) He also urged me to organize a night school for teenagers, for my sake as much as theirs; it would help me in my studies of the language.

The final blow, which I still scarcely believed, came when he confirmed that I would be expected to do the medical work. Mr. Perrett himself had no liking for this aspect of our duties; Mrs. Perrett, who was largely confined to the house by the needs of her invalid daughter, had been doing it all since the departure of George Sach for Makkovik. I was introduced to the apothecary shop and given two elementary books on medicine. After this, I was on my own. I had absolutely no training, though I got some later. Clearly I was going to be very busy.

Pa took me to visit some of the Inuit homes and told me something of each family. Most of the houses were dark and airless, and spoke of extreme poverty. Some were no more than one-roomed shacks. Most were heated by cast iron wood stoves with the trade name "Comfort." I found that in a Labrador winter they offered something less than that, unless you sat close enough to roast your near side.

On my first round of visits I learned that until the turn of the century the Inuit had no surnames. In order to avoid the confusion this created when the village grew in number, they had been encouraged to choose their own family names. Here in Hopedale they had chosen mostly Inuit names, though some chose surnames of English or German.

The nearest home to the Mission house was that of Teofiluse Nitsma and his blind wife Sabina. They had an adopted son, Elias, a man slightly younger than myself, who became my good friend. He took me ptarmigan hunting, and duck egg hunting in the spring. He taught me the use of a rifle and snowshoes. Although he had a good knowledge of English (he had been an interpreter for the Bay at Wolstenholme in the Arctic) he was not really fluent, for his speech was full of odd quirks and nuances which caused me much difficulty at first. Later, when I began speaking his language, our roles were reversed and I gave him many laughs.

As the round of home visits progressed, I had to try to get my tongue around names like Sigsigak (squirrel), Mitsuk (dew), Sillitt (whetstone) and Pijogge, which echoed my own surname in that it meant one who was habitually proud. I soon discovered that the Inuit were calling me *Angutainak*, which means "the man all alone" or "the single man." *Angutainak* I was to remain until I married.

I started teaching on the following morning. Since the school house in Hopedale had been loaned to a homeless family, lessons were held in the mission house, every morning from Monday to Friday. My class, the oldest, was held in my own quarters. I taught the standard subjects, reading, writing and arithmetic. The children seemed to enjoy it, particularly when the older boys mocked my English accent. In the beginning I was frustrated when the children jabbered in Inuktut among themselves, and in reply to my questions. They often went into gales of laughter, which I knew was directed at me. Yet when I tried to make a joke I invariably left them puzzled.

The academic standard was not high. The children were lucky to reach the level of Grade 5, but at least they learned to read and write and do simple arithmetic. I was not an imaginative teacher, though

I hope I helped them a little. Certainly they helped me, especially in my studies of their language.

Much of life in Hopedale was a shock to me at first, as a shy city lad from another land. The absence of plumbing and sanitation was a hardship new to me. In winter, everyone filled their barrels from a water hole three or four hundred yards from the village. In summer, galvanized iron pipes brought water from a small dam to a faucet at the western edge of the community. The two indoor toilets in the mission house were the only ones in town, though two other homes boasted outdoor toilets. Everyone else used chamber pots. Kitchen slops and chamber pots were dumped on the bank overlooking the harbour, and the huskies ate everything. Had they not, the village would have been a scene of indescribable filth. As it was I found it hardly bearable.

Two or three hundred huskies prowled the village night and day. The rising crescendo of their howling kept me awake at night, and woke me in the early morning.

In the porches of many homes, wooden tubs of nauseous-looking seal meat and blubber gave noxious smells. Cleanliness was not next to Godliness here. Yet on Sundays the congregation were very clean and tidy. Indeed many were positively immaculate in white *sillapaks* (anoraks) and hairy-legged, white-bottomed sealskin boots, marvels of workmanship worn only to church and on ceremonial occasions. Most of the women also wore little white knitted church caps, a custom imported from Germany in the early days of the Mission.

Most of the Inuit and settlers, male and female, smoked pipes. A few of the younger men smoked cigarettes. Even children of tender age smoked pipes, a practice which some Inuit believed would make them hardy.

Many things I encountered in these first months were strange to me. One of these was the custom of breast feeding in church. My background had not prepared me for this. I remember seeing one woman nursing a son who seemed to be about three. Later that day I met the same little boy sitting on the church steps, smoking a pipe.

On the whole, the young women were quite pretty and nearly all were modest, despite their reputation among some whites. The girls seemed to enjoy school more than the boys and made better progress. The men, young and old, fetched firewood and hunted. Women and young girls fetched water, cleaned sealskins and fought a discouraging battle with the grease and dirt their men brought into the house. Sometimes, too, they helped in sawing and splitting firewood.

The young men were brash and noisy. One of their favourite sports in the spring was jumping from pan to pan on the ice in the harbour. This called for agility, as the smaller pans would tip or submerge. Sometimes the performers were dumped in the water, but this did not deter them. During my first spring I was invited to join in this sport, but was much too cowardly to do so.

In my first winter among these people I recognized a thin margin between life and death. This was even more frightening when I realized that the health of three hundred people spread along more than one hundred miles of coast was almost entirely in my hands. Though I never shirked my medical duties they became, despite my growing knowledge over the years, an almost unbearable burden.

I wondered what England had ever done for the people here, and why among colonists and the native people there was such a morbid attachment to the United Kingdom and the King. It shocked me that so soon after my departure from England I could find myself so critical of institutions which had once been precious. I was further shocked by my own ignorance, measured now by the demands of my role here, and seriously doubted if the conventional theological college was the best place for training young missionaries.

There were lighter moments. In the centre of the woods at Hopedale the mission had a small garden with some flower beds and a garden house or gazebo. In former days they had held picnics here. Late in June of my first summer Pa Perrett asked me to paper the gazebo, and supplied me with rolls of paper and a bowl of paste, as if I needed nothing more. There were a couple of Newfoundland fishing schooners in the harbour and some of the crew were ashore. Two of them wandered into the garden and watched my struggle with the paste and paper. They made me very conscious of my ineptitude. "Not used to this kind of thing, are you, sir?" one of the fishermen remarked.

"There's no need to rub it in," I retorted.

He commented on my youthful appearance and asked my age. I told him I was twenty-nine, which was evidently much older than I looked.

"It makes a difference when you don't have to work for your living, sir," he concluded. I was completely chagrined.

Extract of the Diary of the House Congregation at Nain in Labradore from Augt 1780 to July 15th 1781 communicated by the Brethrens Society for the Furtherance of the Gospel & to the End of 1781

Sepr. 20th 1780. towards Evening we rejoyced at the safe Arrival of the Amity from Okak in our harbour notwithstanding a thick Fog Br. & Sr. Liebisch who arriv. in the Vessel from Okak came soon on shore glad & thankful that our Saviour had preserved & brought them safe hither through continual Fogs they were Ten days on the way from Okak the Esquimaux David related on the 22 that his Wife and Children had lately been preserved in a very great danger Being among the Islands their Boat lay at Anchor of one of them & the men were all gone on shore the Boat broke loose & his Wife and Children were drove out to sea; they were given up for lost, but Old Nerkingock, who was on another Island seeing the Boat loose & driving, came to their Assistance & his Boat & brought them safe back 25th

3

THE SETTLERS, AND OTHERS

The Inuit are not, of course, the only people living in northern Labrador. There are two Indian bands and a number of "settlers" as well as a small group of whites from outside.

Moravian missions had been established in northern Labrador for twenty-one years before the appearance of the first white settlers. Mission diaries record that in 1792 three settlers had arrived in Kaipokak Bay, near what is now Makkovik. I have been unable to discover who they were, but at least two of them married Inuit women. One of the three was said to have been an unfrocked Roman Catholic priest. Whether this is fact or myth is hard to know. I have been told that his name was De Monte and that Monkey Hill, near Makkovik, is a corruption of his name. It seems equally plausible that the name is a corruption of the French or Spanish word for mountain.

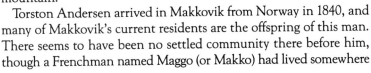

Makkovik 1960

Torston Andersen arrived in Makkovik from Norway in 1840, and many of Makkovik's current residents are the offspring of this man. There seems to have been no settled community there before him, though a Frenchman named Maggo (or Makko) had lived somewhere nearby and had possibly given the place his name. The Moravians did not open a station at Makkovik until 1896, at the invitation of the Andersens. Until then, the nearest mission was at Hopedale, where a mission had been founded in 1782, eleven years after after the founding of Nain.

Like Torsten Andersen, many of the early settlers came to Labrador directly from Europe. Others came via Newfoundland. It is likely that some jumped ship to escape the grim social conditions at home and start fresh in a new land. Others sought asylum from the law, for the laws of England and Newfoundland in that time were terribly harsh and easily breached. So while their courage and desperation brought them to a hostile shore, they found there a freedom they could never have had at home.

It seems strange that although many Irish came to Newfoundland there were none, to my knowledge, in northern Labrador. It may be that the Moravians, with their strong Protestant outlook, discouraged Catholic settlers. There is no evidence of this but neither are there any Irish, while settlers of English and Scottish descent are common.

I arrived in Labrador in the midst of the Depression, when life was nearly as difficult for the settlers as it was for the Inuit. The world market for fur was very depressed, and so was the population of fur bearers. Many of the settlers prided themselves on their self-reliance; the skilled housekeeping of the womenfolk kept many households going even in desperate times. Those who were forced in spite of their pride to accept "poor relief" had a very thin time, for it was poor indeed. They got $1.80 a month for each member of the family, or six cents a day.

In the face of such poverty in the fierce Labrador climate, it was little wonder that many of the people were tuberculous; undernourishment was common. It is true that most people could count on hunting fresh meat in winter, but ammunition took cash and cash was scarce. For that matter, so was the ammunition, all too often, in the Hudson's Bay stores. It is true, however, that most storekeepers were kind and sometimes, like the missionaries, gave help from their own pockets.

On the whole the settlers were more provident and less destitute than the Inuit, and they were better housed. Most were very conscious of their descent from pioneers who, with their hands and little else, had wrested a home and a living from a difficult land.

When I first arrived in Hopedale I found in that region a strong distinction between the races. Those in the village were mostly Inuit, while the majority of settlers dwelt away from the village in the neighbouring bays and inlets. The settlers were called *Kablunangoajut*, or "almost white men," by the Inuit. Whites from the outside were *Kablunat*. About sixty miles north, at Davis Inlet, was a small group of Indians known to the whites as *Naskapi* and to the Inuit as *Allat*. They spent most of their time in the hinterland and came out to the coast only to trade or to visit the priest who came in summer.

Until recently the settlers with Inuit blood were slow to admit it, but this attitude is breaking down. When I first came, some of them lived exactly like the Inuit, while others clung fiercely to their European traditions. They maintained large, well-run homes and had kept many European dishes and customs, though they preserved their meat and fish in the Inuit fashion. At night, they held family prayers and then took up their musical instruments—organ, autoharp, banjo, concertina or violin—for a lively musical evening. Those who could not play, sang. Some, too, were craftsmen of no mean ability, having come out as tradesmen for the Hudson's Bay Company, and struck out on their own when they had served their time.

I did not really get to know any of the settlers in the Hopedale district until I made my first dog team journey to visit them in the little coves where they made their homes. The first of these trips was to Adlatok and Itibliasuk. It was a poor introduction to dog team travel, for my driver was chosen not for his ability but his poverty; he needed the pay. This meant that I, a greenhorn who needed the help and instruction of a good driver, got something less. Josua did his best but showed a very bad temper when the dogs disobeyed. However, he was a likeable little fellow who made up in energy what he lacked in competence.

As we drove up the ice of Adlatok Bay, Josua, who had been instructed to speak only in Inuktut, broke into English long enough to tell me that Uncle Willie Mitchell, whom we were about to visit, must be a millionaire; he even had a piano. Uncle Willie was in fact more prosperous than his neighbours. His house was by far the largest in Adlatok, and he had another in Hopedale, but the Mitchells suffered like everyone else in the Depression.

One of Uncle Willie's daughters lived at home and was about to be married to James Gear, son of the next-door neighbour; I performed the ceremony that spring. Two other daughters, one married to a Newfoundlander named William Oldford and another to Sid Goudie, also lived nearby. The two remaining houses in Adlatok were the homes of Nat and Sandy Gear and their families. These were fine people, very much under the influence of the patriarch, Uncle Willie. His wife, Aunt Tillie, was sister to Nat and Sandy.

When I had finished holding a service and inquiring into the health of my hosts, we sat around and talked. I was anxious to know all I could about life in this remote spot, and I had to be careful not to pry. But the folk here, especially the younger ones, were anxious to learn of England, the home of their ancestors.

That evening the women stretched and turned my sealskin boots, to keep them supple, and dried the duffel liners. Josua made sure that my sleeping bag was stretched out in a warm spot. The bag was of sealskin lined with caribou skin, and was laid out on a polar bear skin. I slept well.

From Adlatok we set out next morning to Itibliasuk, several hours away. There were three homes here, that of my driver Josua, his parents and his brother Mike. How Mike came to be Josua's brother was a mystery to me, the first of many puzzles in northern kinship; Mike's surname was Kemuksigak, while Josua's was Abel. Mike's wife Lizzie was a very attractive Inuit woman from Wolstenholme in the Northwest Territories, where Mike had been an interpreter for the Hudson's Bay. Josua's parents were Inuit but his wife was a settler, a Voisey from Voisey's Bay, near Nain.

That evening just before dark Josua ran excitedly into his father's house and announced the presence of a fox on a hill near the house. He dashed out again, and a minute later we heard the crack of a rifle and a whoop of triumph from Josua, who ran up to claim his prize. He returned, very chagrined, with a dead dog, a small, unfortunate bitch with a rather bushy tail.

On my return to Hopedale, Pa Perrett informed me that later in January I was to visit the settlers north of Hopedale and, with Josua again as my driver, continue on to Nain to meet the superintendent of the Mission, the Reverend Paul Hettasch. It was on this trip that I began to establish a reputation which dogged me everywhere, that of being a jinx for travel.

4

BY DOG TEAM
TO NAIN

My first dog sled trip had been leisurely, short and comfortable. I was hardly prepared for the next, which took more than three weeks of rough going. We travelled nearly three hundred miles through blizzards and deep snow, and over long portages across the necks of land between the frozen bays. It was on this trip that I learned how temperamental Josua could be.

The first day was extremely cold, which made for hard sledding; snow crystals are somehow less slippery in the bitter cold. Josua countered this by "icing" the runners. He took a mouthful of water from a thermos flask and squirted it over the runners, then rubbed the quickly-freezing surface with a duffel mitt. This process had to be repeated before we reached Big Bay Neck, the long portage between Little Bay (Akkellekoluk) and Big Bay Jack Lane's Bay (Kangidlukoluksuk).

The narrow path through the spruce forest along this portage was indescribably beautiful, but it was here that I really saw Josua's limitations as a driver. The track made by earlier travellers wound past tree stumps and bushes which often tangled the traces of our dogs. The poor creatures would almost strangle themselves trying to get free, then give up and lay down in the snow. Josua would run up and beat them with the butt of his whip, or kick them, impatiently dismissing my objections. He insisted a beating was all they understood.

I felt we could avoid much of the trouble if we could watch for snags ourselves. I began to do so, running ahead of the *komatik* to lift the traces over stumps in our path. Josua was not pleased and thought me an ignorant fool for taking this trouble.

It took us nearly all the daylight hours to reach the home of the Broomfields, about twenty-five miles from Hopedale, where we were to spend the first night. The Broomfields lived on the north shore of Big Bay, in a house we could clearly see when we slid down off the portage to the south shore of the frozen bay. As we drew near I studied the large, low, weathered house, with a fine pyramid of firewood piled beside it. Since the Broomfields lived right on the main route from Hopedale to Davis Inlet and Nain, they scarcely spent a week without guests. Everyone who passed by, whether they stopped for a brief visit or were stormbound for days, enjoyed the finest hospitality the home could offer. No one was ever turned away or left unfed.

The blind patriarch of the family was the grandfather, Uncle Sam Broomfield, who was in his seventies. His two proudest possessions were a letter from the equerry of King George VI, thanking him for a sealskin tobacco pouch he had sent on the occasion of the King's Silver Jubilee, and his long service medal from the Hudson's Bay Company, which I believe also paid him a small pension.

His son Walter was a short, powerfully-built man married to Carrie Andersen from Makkovik. Their five children were all at the boarding school there. Later I travelled with Walter by boat and dog team, and I came to regard him as one of the outstanding dog team drivers in northern Labrador. He was so powerful that he could untangle his dogs' traces while underway, a performance that must be seen to be believed. Sitting at the front of the *komatik*, he would haul on the "bridle," the sealskin tow-line to which the traces were attached, until he reached the toggle that secured them. He unhitched them, untangled them, then hitched them again, with one powerful arm serving as the only link between his lunging dogs and the *komatik* during this complex procedure.

The final member of the Broomfield family was Uncle Sam's oldest grandchild by a daughter who was married and living in Nain. John, two years younger than myself, was a most remarkable man—kindly, godly and the finest kind of gentleman. He never married but cared for Walter and Carrie's children when their parents died. He became one of the founders of the town of Happy Valley, where he was known to everyone as Uncle John. When I later moved there he became my helper, my true friend and brother and an inspiration to my ministry.

Late on the evening we arrived at the Broomfields, we were joined by the factor of the Hudson's Bay post in Nain, Dave Massie, and his driver, *en route* to Hopedale. We spent the remainder of the day yarning with the Broomfields about life in Labrador, while a blizzard raged outside and John tirelessly fed the woodstove. Uncle Sam took up his violin from time to time, to play a lively interlude between his stories. The stories themselves were doubtless touched up a little for my amusement and edification.

After evening prayers, the family got out their instruments and we had a spirited songfest of hymns, Scottish airs and English melodies. I strongly suspected the Hudson's Bay man of introducing a little lubricant into the proceedings, but he kept it out of my sight in deference to my calling.

The blizzard continued all the next day so we spent it the same way, in a marathon of song and story. The storm ended that night. The following morning we harnessed the dogs, lashed the *komatiks*, said our farewells and departed, Massie and his driver to the south, Josua and I to the north.

The Broomfield home on Big Bay was adjacent to the trail across Flower's Bay Neck, on the far side of which lay Flower's Bay, or Jem Lane's Bay. This portage revealed a beauty even more lovely than the path we had taken over Big Bay Neck a few days before. There were several "slides" and "overhangs" on our path, which was exciting to a novice like myself. An overhang is a snowdrift built out over a drop in the ground, much like the crest of a wave about to break. A slide is simply a treacherous slope. Some of these hazards called for strenuous effort from all of us, dogs, driver and myself, though I was hampered by my inexperience with snowshoes.

My natural clumsiness, coupled with inexperience and very deep snow, saw me tangled and toppled many times. My irritation was compounded by Josua's obvious skill, and by his digs at me. Patience is a virtue I acquired slowly in my later years; I had little of it here. Theological training barely curbed my tongue. As the morning wore on and the going got worse, I almost wished I had never seen Labrador, but in a few hours I began making progress. By the time we came off the portage I was actually beginning to enjoy the exercise.

Coming down off the neck, we crossed the bay to David Flowers' home. David was a very quiet man but a competent hunter noted for his marksmanship. His several sons were fine hunters and trappers as well, and all the Flowers men were skilled wood carvers. Their exquisite carvings of caribou, especially, helped to supplement the family income. David's wife was a vigorous, somewhat domineering woman, but a very competent housekeeper who saw to it that her daughters matched her in this. We stayed several hours, during which I held a short religious service and conducted my first baptism.

We moved on then through the deep snow towards Davis Inlet, known to the Inuit as Ukkuseksalik, the place of material for cooking pots, or soapstone. Most of our journey lay across the ice of bays and inlets, rather than over land, but progress was painfully slow. The heavy hauling earlier that day was taking its toll. It was quite dark when we eventually arrived at the Hudson's Bay house in Davis Inlet, where we were greeted by Angus Fridge, the young Scots factor. Fridge was a bachelor, but his house was kept by Aunt Lil, a tiny hunchback lady who was a daughter to Uncle Sam Broomfield. She was a fine cook.

After an excellent meal of ptarmigan and vegetables I went to the nearest home to hold service, which had been arranged as the dogs were unhitched. This was the home of Gilbert Saunders, his wife Lilee (another Broomfield), a daughter and six sons, three of whom were in school in Makkovik. Gilbert was the Hudson's Bay Company servant. He was a big man much given to practical jokes, some of which I suffered in later years.

Though the settlers at Davis Inlet were Moravian, the Indians were Roman Catholic. Nevertheless, a number of them came to the service in the Saunders home. Using Gilbert as an interpreter, I explained that although I was a minister I was not of the same faith. Old Edward Rich, the chief, assured me this would not matter.

Early the next morning we left for Sango, home of the Edmunds' family who had returned from Ungava Bay the previous fall. Near Porcupine Head we called at the home of James Saunders, who later became my very good friend. He was hunting but I met Maggie, his wife. We stopped for prayers and promised to call on our return journey, then set out slowly up the bay.

The weather was lovely but the going was tough; we were breaking trail after the blizzard. Heavily-wooded hills stood black and sombre against the dazzling quilt of new snow. Josua was unhappy with the conditions; he proposed that we cache some of our gear and pick it up on our return. This seemed absolute folly to me, for there was no surplus in our load. We could scarcely do without our sleeping bags, extra clothing and the grub box. I refused to consider it.

Just before sunset, despite Josua's dire prophecies, we reached the head of Sango Bay and the Edmunds' home. There were ten living here, in a large and well-built log house erected that fall. Uncle David Edmunds, newly retired from the Hudson's Bay Company, had moved the whole family back from Ungava to his old home in Sango. With him were his wife Emily and their son Albert, and two adopted sons, Norman and John, as well as Albert's Inuit wife Charlotte and their four children.

There is not space to mention all the new and interesting men and women I met on our slow journey to Nain, though we stopped at every home. Many will appear later in this book.

After a pleasant evening and a comfortable night at Sango, we left the next morning across Sango Neck for Okpatik Bay. This portage had not been used in all the years the Edmunds were away, and the route through the forest was overgrown and poorly defined. Albert Edmunds volunteered to guide us. The snow was extremely deep and the way winding. All of us worked hard; Albert broke trail, Josua steered the *komatik* and I struggled behind on snowshoes, plunging forward to help push when the *komatik* bogged down or to right it when it tipped.

We arrived at the home of Herbert Dicker and family late in the evening, having come only a few miles. We were exhausted but very thankful for Albert's help. Without him Josua would surely have been lost and we would have had to work much harder beating our way across the neck. Herbert Dicker was in Nain. He had shot himself through the hand with a .22 caliber rifle, and had gone there for help. Over the years I was amazed at how frequently people shot themselves, usually with .22s. I believe they handled these small weapons carelessly, for wounds from larger weapons were rare.

The next day we visited three homes between Okpatik and Zoar. The first was that of Freeman Saunders, the mail carrier, who lived at Daniel's Rattle with Naomi, his second wife, and a large family of tow-headed children. Freeman was away in Nain, loading up with mail and gossip for his run south. Like all travellers on the coast Freeman carried the news wherever he went, but he dispensed it with more style and relish than most. He was welcome in every home from Nain to Makkovik.

From Daniel's Rattle we had a short and easy run to Tom Gear's, then a brief visit with Alf Ford before we pushed on to Boat Harbour, Zoar.

Chesley Ford, who lived at Zoar, was a remarkable man of many skills who had served both the Moravian Mission and the Hudson's Bay Company. He kept scrapbooks of anything written about

Labrador. He was an exceptional woodworker and I am fortunate to own several of the intricate, inlaid trays and tables for which he was famous.

Hand Crafted Cupboard from Nain

Chesley had a reputation among the mission staff for being rather "wild." One of his escapades had enlivened the dedication of a new church after the disastrous fire in Nain in 1924. Two cannons had been given to the Mission by the government 150 years before, for reasons which escape me. Several young men, led by Chesley, decided to contribute a one-gun salute to the dedication service. The bishop was not amused, and ordered the cannons buried. Forty-five years later, during the celebration of the Mission's bicentennial in Nain, the cannons re-emerged from the clay.

Chesley's wife Mary was equally tough and resourceful, scarcely hindered by an artificial leg. Shortly after their marriage she had injured her foot while trapping. Chesley was unable to leave his work and had hired a dog team to take her to the Mission hospital at Okak.

It was a long journey in very bad weather; her leg needed amputation by the time they arrived. After her recovery, she continued to hunt and trap near her home. Like so many of the settler women, Mary was an excellent cook. Over the years I travelled the coast, she gave me some of the best meals I have ever eaten.

As we moved north from Boat Harbour the country grew more stark and forbidding, but travelling conditions improved. We stopped briefly at Annaksakarusek, about eight miles from Zoar, to visit an Inuit family named Noa, then set out over the ice across the mouth of Voisey's Bay. Josua became animated and happy as we approached the end of our journey. However, I was impatient, and found these last few miles tedious. The outer islands in the bay looked very grim and the distant hills of the mainland seemed to retreat as we approached them.

About halfway across the mouth of the bay we spotted a *komatik* approaching us from the north. It was my friend from the *Kyle*, Corporal Frank Mercer of the Newfoundland Rangers. He was heading south to Hopedale to radio St. John's with news of an alleged murder at Okak. I was shortly to meet the accused.

Nain 1940

5

NAIN AND THE
JOURNEY BACK

At Nain I was greeted by the superintendent of the Mission, Paul
Richard Hettasch, whose job I would take over five years later. He
was of German extraction, though born to Moravian missionary parents in South Africa. Well educated, refined, and renowned on the
coast for his medical ability, he was of the old mission school, a stern
and totally unbending moralist. He did not, however, deserve the
cruel caricature of the missionary villain portrayed by a Newfoundland novel based on events taking place at about this time.

Paul Hettasch's wife, Ellen, had been born in the Rhineland and
still had, unlike Paul, a heavy German accent. "Tante" Hettasch was
a typical German housewife who confined her interests to the home
and had little to do with the Inuit residents of the village. Her daughter, Katie, and Friede Glaser made up the remainder of the mission
"family" at that time.

The Newfoundland Rangers, Frank Mercer and Ed English, had
been unable to reach their post at Hebron before freeze-up and had
therefore joined Constable Maurice Christian in Nain. With them
was Esau Gillingham who was being held on a charge of murder.

I came to know Gillingham as a remarkable man. Charming, tough
and immoral, he was a memorable fellow but he was not the gallant
figure some describe. Generally speaking, he exploited the Inuit and
had little real respect for them. Though a prisoner, Gillingham was
quite free to visit in the village. In fact he was little more than a

boarder who shared the Rangers' quarters. He and Richard White were cronies; Gillingham visited him daily. Ultimately the case against him was dismissed. He left Labrador to live in Newfoundland and was, I understand, drowned while fishing. His canoe was found floating upside down.

Nain is built at the foot of a hill which rises eight hundred feet above the village. Across the bay stand two higher and more forbidding hills, which in winter always seem almost black against the ice of the harbour. Their faces rise sheer from the tiny beaches below, and their slopes support nothing more than a few scraggy bushes and moss. In the depth of winter they throw their shadow over the village for much of the day. These two menacing hills bear the names Sophia and Maria, and were evidently named for the wives of missionaries. I have sometimes wondered if the women deserved it.

Our journey to Nain had been difficult, but in the bright sunshine of our departure, Josua assured me the return trip would be easy; we were going south. Scarcely an hour later, when we had barely rounded the southern point of the bay, it began to snow. Very soon the wind rose and we were in the midst of a minor blizzard. It might have been wiser to return to Nain but that soon became impossible, for Josua was now hopelessly lost.

After wandering around almost six hours in a "whiteout," where the light is so diffused by falling or drifting snow that shadows and therefore all clues of shape and distance vanish from the landscape, we came ashore through rough ice to low land with forest behind. Immediately we heard the din of dogs. Continuing up the shore a short way we came to a small cabin, the dogs of which joined ours in a great hullaballoo. This brought the occupants to their door.

They were Henoche Saksagiak and his wife Amalia, who had come here to Paul's Island from Nain to trap. They welcomed us warmly, but the blizzard kept us there three days in their cluttered, one-room shack. They were not comfortable days, and I thought often of the relative luxury of the mission house in Nain, scarcely seven miles away. Amalia, a very big woman, spent much of our visit plying me with questions, which challenged my still meagre command of Inuktut.

Finally the storm broke and we left just after daybreak in mild weather. We had not gone far before a thick fog settled over the ice. Soon we were lost again, wandering aimlessly through fog. Twice we came back on our own tracks. Finally we crossed an old trail, the track of someone who had known where he was going, and we followed it.

That evening, just at sunset, we reached the home of a man I shall not name, and his wife and two sons. The man had apparently been prosperous when he was younger, for he had employed maid servants to help his wife. The maids were the mothers of his sons. The elder son was nicknamed the "judge" because, it was claimed, some visiting dignitary had granted him this authority.

Their cabin, lacking a maid now, was not clean. The woman was quite frail and several times during our visit almost fell to the floor. The "judge" took me aside and confided that he too was sick, especially when the north wind blew. On these occasions he treated his mother cruelly, often hitting her with his fist. I had heard something of his reputation already, and was warned that he was a schemer. I could not be sure if he was scheming now, or was genuinely repentant. In any case, I talked with him and prayed with him, and there the matter stood.

There was an air of evil about that place and as the years passed I felt it with every visit. When the father died in curious circumstances, his sons and his wife burned the house and moved to Nain. The "judge" told me they burned the place because it was evil, a sentiment I could readily accept.

The following day we made good time to Boat Harbour. This was a mere six miles, but threatening weather kept us there overnight. I was glad of a chance to see more of Chesley Ford and to harvest some of his vast knowledge of Labrador. He was an excellent organist and, like so many in that country, a philosopher. While he appreciated the efforts of the Moravian Mission over the years, he was also critical; he felt some missionaries were excessively harsh with "sinners." So did I, and Chesley's views helped me in my job when I became superintendent many years later. It was a rich experience for a young missionary to talk with Chesley, and I have always valued the friendship I had with this family.

Chesley had immense energy and a great deal of family pride. One of his sons was married to an Inuk and was manager of a Hudson's Bay post in the Arctic. Another was later an interpreter for the RCMP. Thirty-two years after I first met them, it was a joy for Doris and me to take Chesley's great-grandson on a visit to England, a small payment on the debt we owe that fine family.

From boat harbour we moved quickly along to Okpatik Bay and the home of Young David Edmunds. Young David, like many other settlers, had served the Hudson's Bay in the Arctic and had taken an Inuk wife. Annie was even less sophisticated than the Labrador

Inuit. Their home was dark and dismal, though unlike many it had two rooms. A husky bitch wandered freely through the house, snatching food when it could.

A few years later on a trip with Doris we stopped for the night at this home. The Edmunds had run out of oil for their lamp and had no candles. Since I always carried them, we lit a few to give Doris enough light to cook us all a meal of corned beef hash. When she turned aside for a moment the dog snatched the meal right from the pan. Later that night the bitch gave birth to thirteen puppies, which softened our hearts a little.

Continuing south we stopped for the night at Daniel's Rattle, Freeman Saunders' home. Freeman was still somewhere between Makkovik and Davis Inlet, carrying mail. One of Freeman's many children was a boy named Alan who died tragically ten years later, together with Johnnie Ford, a grandson of Chesley. They were lost in a blizzard which lasted several days, but a week had passed before we in Nain knew they were missing. We began the search on the morning of the eighth day, Lieutenant Clarke of the Newfoundland Rangers, George Dicker, Dan Henoche and I. When we found the boys they were both dead from exposure and the dogs had half eaten Johnnie. It was obvious that Alan had given his life in an effort to save his friend. Alan's body was fully clothed but his sleeping bag, and the boy's blankets, were wrapped around his younger companion.

We made very good time the next day and reached Big Bay and another warm welcome from the Broomfields. Again they brought out their instruments and we had another song-fest after evening prayers. The following day we made a detour into Big Bay to visit John Lane, his wife and three sons in their picturesque home on an island about five miles from the Broomfields. Lavinia, Lane's wife, was a daughter of old Sam. Two of the Lane boys, Sam and Abraham, were off tending their traps; no hunter could afford to sit around waiting for a visit from the missionary. The third and youngest son, Arthur, who was handicapped, was home caring for his parents, a role that later became impossible when his brothers died and his aging parents were overwhelmed with grief. Both brothers died tragically. Indeed, Abraham drowned later in the year of our visit, shooting rapids in a nearby river.

The scenery as we travelled still deeper into the bay was startlingly beautiful. The air was crisp and cold and the dogs were lively, enjoying their work as much as we. About mid-day we reached the homes of Andrew and Jim Lane and their families. Andrew and his son, as well as Jim and his, had just returned from cutting firewood and hunting ptarmigan. The Lanes seemed very poor, and Andrew confided that he found it almost impossible to buy clothes. I promised I would get him some and was able to do so a few weeks later.

After holding a service we started back out the bay toward Broomfields', calling in at the island to say hello to young Sam and Abraham, who had just returned from their traps. After a brief chat we continued on to Uncle Sam's, to another night of yarns and fiddle music followed by a good sleep.

The next morning started clear but soon began to cloud over. By the time we slid off the portage to the ice of Little Bay it was snowing heavily and blowing hard. Soon we were moving through a complete whiteout, a sensation which has been compared to that of an ant trapped in a ping-pong ball. Josua admitted that he was lost but felt that if we continued in the direction we were moving we must soon strike land. When I checked his hunch against my compass I found we were heading straight out toward the edge of the ice, the *sina*. Josua reluctantly admitted the compass might be right.

After several hours on a new course we still did not reach land, but finally I saw through the murk the faint outline of a hill to the west. Josua affected not to see it or to understand me, but after a time he turned the dogs in that direction and we soon struck land. Here he recognized familiar ground, which allowed us to set out in some confidence with a compass bearing for the next leg of our journey. Soon after dark we passed through Black Heads, north of Hopedale, and a few hours later rounded the point of Hopedale Harbour.

The whole trip had taken a little more than three weeks. It was the first of many dog team journeys I was to make, not the longest in miles or duration but an excellent introduction to this form of travel. I was glad to get a bath and climb into my own bed, so much softer than the cold, hard floors on which I had spent most of the last twenty-odd nights. Looking back over the journey from the comfort of my bed, I could not help but sympathize with Josua, my first tutor in Labrador winter travel.

Old Sod House   Hebron 1941

6

THE MISSIONARY
TASK

I had now been in Labrador four months and was only beginning to understand what was expected of a missionary. I had been well trained theologically. I knew all about the many heresies which had rocked the church but not destroyed it. I had a good background in church history. I was proficient in Greek and was a moderately able preacher. I had at one point even taken a course in the wholesaling of food, so I knew a great deal about tea, coffee, cheese, butter and dried fruit. I had been an avid reader from my early childhood and had learned a lot from reading, though some of it was trivial. And I knew my Bible.

But in those days, half a century ago, theological school gave us no insights into the human problems of the poor, the underfed, the sick and the overburdened. I felt it was ironic to preach that Jesus was the bread of life to people with empty bellies. I did not dismiss the relevance of the Christian message even to the hungry, but I could not understand the belief that bibles were more important than food. I was convinced the Gospel must be a social gospel, bringing not only comfort to the soul but deliverance from physical misery as well.

At that time my salary was just over seventy-two dollars a month, out of which I paid forty dollars for board. Yet this was riches compared to those around me, and during my years in Labrador I "loaned" far more than I could really afford and at times gave clothes off my own back. I counted this a small part of my Christian duty and knew that the Inuit would do the same for me.

While the primary task of the missionary was to preach and to live the Gospel, his role included many functions which today are handled by others. The missionary was a welfare officer, doctor and frequently a teacher and school administrator. Often, too, he was an advocate, intervening on behalf of the Inuit with traders, police and sometimes government itself. I shall have more to say of this later.

Until 1935 the missionaries had been largely responsible for policing their communities. This continued even after 1935 in Hebron and Nutak, though they were assisted by a visiting policeman and the *AngajoKauKattiget* or village council.

This group deserves some explanation. From early days the missionaries appointed leading Inuit converts to be chapel servants or church helpers, a role which gave them some authority in the community. In 1907, the organization of the congregation was made more democratic by the election of elders chosen from among the males over twenty-one. One elder was elected for every hundred in the village population. The elders, together with the appointed chapel servants, formed the *AngajoKauKattiget*. After 1953, women were permitted to seek election as elders. I am proud of my own role in bringing this about for it met some resistance from the men. Progress on this front can be seen in the fact that twenty-three years later a woman, Fran MacIntosh, was elected president of the Labrador Inuit Association.

Missionaries were also expected to arrange adoptions through the *AngajoKauKattiget* and to settle family disputes. This traditional system was not challenged until 1939, when a Newfoundland Ranger interfered in a case of custom adoption, an ancient Inuit practice of sharing children with childless friends, or with relatives whose children were grown. A very small child in Nain had been given up by his parents, but when he was fourteen and capable of useful work they wanted him back. The child considered his adoptive parents as his own, and the *AngajoKauKattiget* supported him in this view.

The Ranger insisted the council's action was not "legal." Neither was it illegal, for there was in fact no formal system of adoption in the province at that time. Nevertheless, the Ranger returned the boy to his natural parents. Such meddling and disregard for established local practice can destroy harmony between races. I believed strongly there was no reason why local custom should not prevail, but I was not the superintendent and my superior was not prepared to oppose the Ranger.

It was also the duty of a missionary to learn the language. I devoted every moment I could to the study of Inuktut. Indeed, I had scarcely been in Labrador six weeks when I was instructed to read the litany in that language at the morning service every other Sunday, which meant I spent hours with a chapel servant in preparation.

Upon my return from the northern sled journey in late February, 1936, Pa Perrett told me that he expected me to preach my first sermon in Inuktut on the first Sunday in April. I had been dabbling at writing little pieces in my new language, but now I got down to business. I chose to preach on the text, "Thy kingdom come," perhaps because it was short and I thought it should be simple. The result, which was at least brief, got more attention than it deserved, for the Inuit were models of courtesy.

I was glad to have the opportunity to preach in Inuktut so soon after my arrival, and resolved that in my future preaching I would strive for high standards in my use of that language. Today, half a century later, I deplore the prevalence of bad grammar and sloppy use of Inuktut. The purity of a remarkable language is being destroyed by the ignorant and the lazy.

From the time I became superintendent of the Mission in 1941 until my retirement thirty years later, I was constantly pleading with government on behalf of the Inuit and settlers. It was not always possible for government to help, but I got a sympathetic hearing from all levels of government both before and after Confederation. I am sure authorities did not always understand the problems I brought to them, but they did me the courtesy of listening and assisted as far as they were able. Mr. Smallwood had, I believe, a deep sympathy for the plight of the Inuit but his government had little money for the work required. This changed when federal funding for work in native communities became available.

7

NAIN

In August of 1936, after ten months in Hopedale studying Inuktut and learning something of the local culture, I was transferred to Nain to serve as assistant to the superintendent of the Mission, the Reverend Paul Hettasch. Because the superintendent lived there, Nain was in some respects the capital of northern Labrador and the hub of the life of the Moravian community. This became even more true later.

During my stay in Hopedale I had learned a few useful skills and many important lessons about life in this sub-Arctic land. I spent some time snowshoeing, hunting and, on one occasion, collecting the eggs of eider ducks, highly prized as an addition to the local diet and not, in those days, forbidden fruit. Perhaps the most important lesson of that time, one I continued to learn over the next thirty-five years, was that the weather ruled everything. The best of plans, the most sophisticated technology must frequently yield to wind, fog, blizzards or bad ice.

Hopedale was a barren spot with only a few trees to relieve the nakedness of its surroundings. Nain, though ninety-five miles farther north and very close to the limit of trees, was more wooded, being set back farther from the frigid Labrador Current which sweeps the outer coast. In spite of the forbidding hills, Sophia and Maria, Nain seemed a less desolate place where life might be easier than in Hopedale. The activities were the same; the houses were much the same; the basic terms of life were similar; but Nain could boast of better sealing places, better caribou hunting and better trapping, and firewood was not twenty miles away.

There was also more of an Inuit "flavour" to Nain; its people were less touched by the ways of white men. It was not until 1936 that

Nain had radio contact with the Marconi station at Hopedale, and through Hopedale, with the outside world. This was a tenuous link, sometimes lost for as much as a week at a time. Reception of commercial radio stations was equally erratic. The signal was most likely to fade, of course, at a crucial point in a news broadcast. It was difficult to pick up Newfoundland radio stations, but Radio Moscow came in clearly most days.

There were very few settlers in Nain itself and they lived at the west end of the village, while the Inuit lived farther along the shore to the east. I never did fully understand this division, but I was told it had existed from the earliest days of white settlement. The Mission owned the land in the community, on a grant going back to its foundation; anyone wishing to build had to lease land from the Mission and pay "ground rent" of ten cents a year. The missionary would normally discuss such an application with the elders, the *AngajoKauKattiget*. I personally objected to the village being segmented as it was and over the years managed to get some integration of Inuit and settler housing, but I never did succeed in getting a settler to build at the eastern end of the village.

The Mission in Nain had a large vegetable garden, much more prolific than the garden in Hopedale. This was perhaps chiefly because its soil had been lovingly collected from all around the station, wherever small pockets of soil could be found. Long daylight hours made up for the short summer season, so that a period of quick, intense growth was possible. Our produce would not have won ribbons at a country fair, but the garden gave us many of our vegetables. Quick growing species like lettuce and radish did extremely well. Crops like cabbage, carrots and cauliflower were highly dependent on weather. One crop which never failed, which supplied not only the entire village but the crews of visiting schooners, was rhubarb.

The summer I was transferred to Nain the garden was exceptionally good, and I recall writing Doris an enthusiastic letter about it. I had never been keen on gardening myself, but I knew she was, so I was glad to pass on news of the opportunities here. In Hopedale I had helped Natan Friede start a garden, but none of the Inuit in Nain seemed interested; gardening was a missionary pursuit. However, I was glad to learn that many of the settlers who lived in the bays had good gardens.

In Hopedale, while I had been helped and guided by Pa Perrett, I had felt fully his partner in the work of our church. In Nain, however, I was under the direct supervision of the superintendent,

Paul Hettasch, and felt very much the junior missionary. Although I had a fairly large, sparsely furnished house to myself, I ate with the others: Paul, his wife Tante Hettasch, and the two teachers Kate Hettasch and Friede Glaser. In this household I chafed under unwritten, archaic rules of conduct which seemed petty and unreasonable to a restless young man of twenty-nine.

One source of minor discord between Paul Hettasch and myself was my friendship with Richard White, an independent trader who ran a small store in competition with the Hudson's Bay. A well-educated man, then married to his second Inuit wife, Richard had not enjoyed good relations with the missionaries over the years. Just after my arrival I received a short note asking if he might visit that evening. We had, of course, already met, because he lived scarcely one hundred yards away. I replied that I would be glad to receive him, but Reverend Hettasch was not pleased with this news.

I was not deterred, and we spent a very pleasant evening together. I found White very easy to talk to, and full of knowledge of the Inuit and Indians. I did not always agree with his views, for he had a rather worldly outlook and often saw things in terms of profit and loss while I, of course, had other priorities.

White was one of the few men who knew much about the Indians of northern Labrador, even now perhaps the most remote and least integrated Indian band in the country. He gathered information about them for Dr. F.G. Speck, author of *Naskapi, the Savage Hunters of the Labrador Peninsula*, and collected artifacts and clothing and indeed anything pertaining to their culture for Dr. Speck.

During the next two winters, White visited my home almost every week for a discussion on a subject of his choosing. On the morning of his visit I would receive a note which specified the subject of our talk, which of course gave him quite an edge in debate. These themes would often centre around a quotation, and they ranged from politics to religion, from life to death. White liked to summarize our debates at the end, but he was always scrupulously fair and would admit defeat when he was beaten, which was more than I could do. At half his age, I was more reluctant to concede.

On one occasion, I silenced him completely. He was saying that the training of clergy was too unworldly; it left them ill-equipped to meet the challenges of the world. Perhaps to his surprise, I quite agreed. Hoping to shock me, he went on to say that every young theology student should be compelled to read *Lady Chatterley's Lover*, at that time a banned book. I told him I had already read it. Reaching

ing for the high ground, he remarked that he had heard of a new book, a real sizzler called *Forever Amber*. When I offered to lend it to him, he gave up and changed the subject.

We were never close friends, but we had a happy relationship over the years and a good deal of mutual respect. Two years later, while I was in Makkovik, Richard White moved his establishment from Nain to Kauk Bight because of some disagreement with the Mission. When I returned to Nain in 1941, a married man by then, Doris and I visited his home in Kauk a number of times. We were always received with the kindness and courtesy he had shown me in previous years.

He was living in Kauk when I was summoned to his bedside one afternoon with the news that he was dying. I walked the four or five miles through the gloom of early darkness to Kauk Bight. There was little I could do other than give him some slight relief from pain. A day or two later he died. He was missed by the Indians and Inuit to whom he had many times offered hospitality and aid.

My first two years in Nain were not particularly happy ones. This probably contributed to the stomach trouble which began after about six months and which plagued me for the next thirty-odd years. So many things were off-limits to a single young missionary. Brother and Sister Hettasch were very kind, but they were steeped in traditions which seemed to me to be hindering the Mission and which seemed over-protective of the Inuit and myself. Though I had never thought of myself as a rebel, I had strong views and suffered now by the need to suppress them.

I would have been utterly miserable without the friendship of the Newfoundland Ranger, Maurice Christian, and his wife Bobby. Yet even this association was misunderstood. Reverend Hettasch did not see any need for friendships outside "the Mission family," while I needed less stifling company.

One of my tasks at Nain was to maintain the thirty-two-volt Delco lighting plant which supplied power to both mission houses and the church. It may be clear to the reader by now that there were many practical things I could not easily master. One of these was the internal combustion engine. The generator was unpredictable, at best, and its wet batteries were not designed for the hard use we gave them. So the operation and maintenance of this lighting plant was a nightmare, and would have driven me crazy without the help of Maurice Christian.

I spent long hours coaxing, wheedling and mucking about with that engine. In the little unheated engine house, at temperatures of minus thirty Fahrenheit, the cold and frustration drove me to despair. At times the lights would fail in the middle of a church service, and if I was conducting the worship I would be compelled to leave the service or cut it short, or carry on with flashlights. In either case, I was doomed to more struggle with that hated machine, which strained my patience and endangered my immortal soul. The irony is that there were many Inuit in the congregation who would have been delighted to operate the lighting plant and who would surely have done it more ably than I, but who were not permitted to do so.

Following my first winter in Nain, Admiral Donald B. MacMillan, an explorer who frequently called in at Nain and became a very good friend of the Mission, presented us with a thirty-two-volt Wind-charger. This instrument gave us cheap power when the wind blew, but was something of a hazard when it blew too fiercely, for the blades were mounted on a sixty-foot tower. However, it was of considerable help and saved me some hours of misery in the engine house.

My visits to people around the bays were always enjoyable, though my stomach was now giving me great trouble and I had bouts of vomiting after almost every meal. By this time I was preaching in Inuktut every other Sunday, and although my material must have been poor, the Inuit seemed to appreciate my sermons and were most encouraging.

The village of Nain was and no doubt still is the home of a number of very remarkable people, members of a remarkable race.
One who awed me was
Martin Martin, the chief
elder. He was from Okak,
a survivor of the hideous flu
epidemic of 1918 which
wiped out a community
begun in 1776. He was
an outstanding per-
sonality, respected
by all who knew
him. To me he
epitomized the
Inuit race; he was
Inumarik, the complete, the
whole, the absolute Inuk. When he spoke,
all stopped to listen, for he was eloquent and slightly aggressive. He

was the champion of his people but he hated injustice, whoever the victim. His dominating and yet merciful personality put its stamp on the Inuit religious community, while in his prowess as a hunter he towered over others. He was bitterly opposed to the use of alcohol by the Inuit because of its degrading effects on his people. He was not only chairman of the village council but the leading Inuit voice in church affairs, and recognized as such not just in Nain, but the whole region. He was a strong man in every sense.

His wife Benigna was even stronger. On our first meeting, she seemed rather remote, but as our acquaintance ripened I came to know her as a warm and friendly person. She was by far the best bootmaker in Nain, but she confined her craft to her immediate family, who were always the best shod in the community. Many years after our first meeting, when Martin and I had travelled many miles together and I was a frequent visitor to their home, Benigna looked at my feet and asked bluntly, "Who made your boots?" I told her, and thought nothing more about it. A little later she came to our home and thrust a beautifully-made pair of boots into my hands saying, "These are for you." I knew then that I belonged, and we grew closer over the years. In time Martin became not merely my driver and friend, but my Inuit father.

Sealskin boots are marvels of ingenuity. A triumph in the clever application of local materials, (the snowhouse is another) they remain the best winter footwear in the north even today, when mail order shoppers have access to nearly every form of boot the world can offer. Unlike the "barked" or home-tanned boots of southern Labrador, the traditional Inuit skin boots are completely waterproof. This is achieved by not removing the black epidermis when preparing the skin, by using sinew for thread (which swells when damp and plugs the holes made by the needle), and by a stitching technique which pierces only the tough outer surface of the

Kamik

hide. The barked boots of southern Labrador and the white-bottomed boots the Inuit wear to church are supple and handsome, but practical only in cold, dry snow. The only drawback to the black, waterproof skin boots is that they need continual care, softening and stretching them each night, or they become as stiff as plywood.

Another remarkable man in Nain was Isaak Rich. Isaak had never been an elder but was a prominent member of the *AngajoKauKattiget*, the church and village council. He was an extremely vocal man despite a slight speech impediment which became more pronounced when he was excited. This was frequent, for Isaak found life itself exciting and had a thirst for knowledge which I have not seen equalled among the Inuit. As he talked he would gesture vigorously, while his grey bobbed hair shook like the mane of a lion.

Before I had my radio station, I would gather a summary of the world news and translate it into Inuktut for Isaak. On Sunday morning after church he would gather as many as thirty people into his small house and would read from the news I had compiled, liberally adding his own comments and interpretations.

Although he was past seventy, Isaak was always the last hunter to return before breakup in the spring, causing everyone much anxiety when he lingered at the hunt while the ice grew rotten and treacherous. After one such time I scolded him gently for worrying his wife, Hedwig. His mane shook and his grey moustache bristled as he retorted, "Do you think I am a man or a mouse?" It was as if he meant that only a *Kablunak* would suggest that a great hunter stay home because of the softness of a woman.

But Hedwig was hardly soft. Though even older than Isaak and almost blind, she was very vigorous. She did not get outdoors often but rarely missed church, and always during the winter wore a pair of caribou skin pants beneath a voluminous skirt, topped off with an equally bulky *artiga*, or parka.

She was the only woman in Nain who could remember using a seal skin bucket, or sewing a kayak, a team project she herself had supervised when she was young. When Isaak was away, the old lady often sat rocking and singing softly to herself. The songs were those of her childhood and youth, and included the songs that women sewing kayaks would sing together. I persuaded her to let me record them. I made the recording on a magnetic wire system, a clumsy, heavy and irritating forerunner to the tape recorder, but I got a good copy despite the limitations of that equipment. Unhappily I never got around to translating and transcribing her songs, and still more unhappily the recording itself was lost during our move to Happy Valley in 1957. I was deeply upset, for Hedwig was probably the last woman in Labrador to know those songs.

A third man who impressed me during my first two years in Nain was Abia Green. He too was blind and a church elder. Despite reports of a somewhat lurid youth, he was an uncompromising moralist and took a vigorous interest in all the affairs of the village.

His wife, Regina, was another remarkable Labrador woman. The only time I ever saw her without a pipe in her mouth was in church. While she was not at all masculine, and in fact was a slim, good-looking woman, she could do nearly everything a man could do, doubtless to compensate for Abia's blindness. As a measure of her competence, she and her daughter Hulda, after Abia's death, built a cosy little cottage by themselves. Regina had a rather rough tongue and was prone to speaking out vigorously on public affairs, which in Nain were normally the business of men.

In my first years in Nain, life was by no means easy for those who earned their living from the land and sea. This can be precarious anywhere, but in northern Labrador, life in those years was especially hard. The fishing season lasted only about ten weeks and the fisherman's price for salted cod was around two dollars a quintal (112 pounds). The fisherman was caught in an almost hopeless struggle just to recover the costs of his operation. Trapping, too, was a chancy occupation, with little return for days of strenuous effort. Dwindling markets had reduced the price for fox pelts, while the proliferation of fox and mink farms introduced new competition. Hunting, the other main pursuit, is by nature a game of chance but especially so in the north, where weather is harsh and fickle and the migratory habits of game can change radically without notice.

So it was that these hardy hunters were engaged in a battle of wits and perserverence. The longer I lived among them the greater was my admiration for their skills, adaptability, patience and fortitude, and above all their amazing resilience in the face of difficulty, frustration and disaster.

Visiting the homes of my parishioners, I always felt ashamed of the comparative comfort of the mission house, yet I was poor compared with the storekeepers, police and others from "outside."

The Inuit, young and old, were frequent visitors to my bachelor home. It always delighted me that even the most hardened, experienced hunters had a quality of wonder and curiosity in their make-up. Some things were so far outside their experience that they were beyond comprehension. How, for example, could I convey what it is like to stand with a crowd of sixty thousand, roaring at the tying goal in a soccer cup match, to people who had spent their lives in small family camps and lived now in a village of four hundred.

Despite the vast gulf of experience between us, we never lacked topics of communication, and there was no blaring radio, stereo or television to distract us. Sometimes, though, we sat together in my home and enjoyed the gramophone. My guests would listen with rapt attention to Grieg or Schubert, for the Labrador Inuit are unique among native people in the depth of their exposure to classical music. Their ancestors responded with enthusiasm to the early Moravian emphasis on music, so that for almost two hundred years, Bach chorales and other classics have been part of their heritage. But when I put on a Gilbert and Sullivan recording, or a lively tune from one of the light operas, the mood would change; feet would tap and heads would nod time to the music.

Often friends would borrow my gramophone and a few records for special events like weddings and birthdays, which are red letter days among the Inuit.

In addition there were the church festivals: Young Men's Day, Children's Day, Young Women's Day, Widow's Day and Married Folks' Day. These festivals were originally intended to point out the relationship between each group and their religious obligations, but over the years they had become more than that. Now they included feasts, singsongs and even dances, and a chance for the groups to appear in their brightest formal clothing. They would march to church in a body for morning and afternoon service, and the rest of the community would join them in the late afternoon for a final service. The rest of the day was given over to jollity and feasting. The Hudson's Bay Company looked with some disfavour on these celebrations, which took men away from trapping; but apart from their religious significance they were a welcome break in a long winter.

It was a great day for young people when they first celebrated Young Men's Festival or Young Women's Festival at the age of thirteen. It seemed that these were something more than a Christian ceremony; they were an Inuit initiation into adulthood. As a missionary I took part in all these festivals, but as a bachelor I was an active participant in the Young Men's Festival, marching with the others to church and attending their feasts. The Union Jack was always prominent on these occasions, proudly carried into church by the youngest of the group in the morning and the oldest in the evening.

46

These festivals followed the same pattern year after year, and any change was greeted with protest. The older Inuit were conservative folk, particularly in matters relating to church life. Any suggested change was carefully researched and pondered at length before a decision was made. As I grew older, changes I suggested were regarded with less suspicion and looked upon with the tolerance usually reserved for the aged; but in my early years the combination of youth and bachelorhood did not give me much standing.

At the beginning of my second year at Nain a young woman named Nora Mowl replaced the teacher Friede Glaser, who was returning to Holland on furlough. I had known Nora as the girl friend of a fellow student in theological college, but he had jilted her and gone to the West Indies so she offered her service as a teacher in Labrador. She was a vivacious, plump little blonde woman, but although we knew each other quite well we did not see much of each other even in the little village of Nain. The teachers worked hard, because they ran the boarding home as well as the school, and Nora was not happy during her first year at Nain. At the end of her first year and my second, we were both transferred to Makkovik. Here she met a Newfoundland Ranger from Hopedale, Dean Bragg, whom she married at the end of the school year. Dean was transferred to Nain, and a year later Nora died in childbirth.

In February, 1938, I was transferred back to Hopedale for a few months. Fred Grubb, whom I had replaced temporarily when I first came to Labrador, had taken over the station when Pa Perrett retired. Grubb had been in Labrador since 1919, and was out on furlough in 1934-35. His wife's illness had prevented his return at the end of this period, and this was the emergency which had provoked my hasty and unexpected posting to Labrador that year. Now, early in 1938, I was sent to Hopedale to assist him, for his wife had died in January.

Grubb had served with the Coldstream Guards, a crack British regiment, during World War I. A tall, practical and powerful man with a military bearing, he was now plagued with rheumatism. It was he who had learned to make dentures from a Harvard dental professor and who in turn taught others, including me.

That summer I returned to Nain to pack my possessions for a transfer to Makkovik, where I was to take over from the Reverend George Sach who was returning to England with his family on furlough. In Makkovik, I would have sole charge of the mission station and the boarding school, and though it was only a temporary position

I felt that at last I was free to face the challenge which had brought me to Labrador.

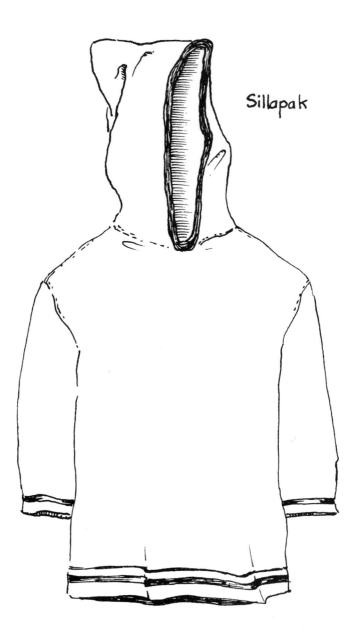

Sillapak

8

MAKKOVIK,
ENGLAND
AND MARRIAGE

When I transferred to Makkovik in 1938, I was received with much kindness and perhaps some apprehension by my new congregation. They knew, of course, that this was the first mission of which I would have sole charge and that the health of the community would now depend on a rank amateur. Nevertheless, I was given much encouragement by young and old. During the following year I found Wilson Andersen, head of the Andersen clan and chief chapel servant, a source of strength and much good advice. One great service was that he sometimes came to me for advice, a tremendous boost to my confidence. He was a quiet-spoken man of Norwegian descent with a deep love of God and an almost fierce devotion to his church. I never once heard him raise his voice in anger or command, but his fishing crew was quick to obey his quiet bidding. Mistakes or offences failed to ruffle his calm, but he would not tolerate injustice or unkindness. He was humble but not obsequious, and he made no virtue of his humility. He was a good man for a friend, and a friend to everyone.

His wife, Harriet, was equally quiet and capable. In contrast to Wilson, who was slim and distinctly Norwegian-looking, Harriet was short and plump, with strong Inuit features.

In addition to their children, Wilson's sister Bertha lived with them. Aunt Bertha was a tallish lady who had never married but rendered great service as the community's midwife. She was not as quiet as her brother, but shared his humour and his family devotion.

Wilson was one of several brothers who must have made life pretty lively for their family when they were growing up. One brother, John, was still alive and living in Makkovik. A brother named Willie, now dead, had been the practical joker of the family. On one occasion he stuffed a little gunpowder in John's pipe. John was a great talker and kept putting his pipe down while he talked, then relighting it when he paused. This, of course, greatly heightened the tension for Willie as he watched. When the explosion came, it blew the pipe to bits. I did not hear what passed between Willie and John in the next few moments.

The Andersen family had founded the village of Makkovik, which was strung out along the shoreline of a bay about fifty miles southeast of Hopedale. Behind the village and around the harbour was a range of high, heavily-wooded hills. The mission premises were at the eastern end of the community and the home of Albert Mitchell was at the other.

There were only two Inuit living in Makkovik at that time: Josua Atsertatajok Xenia, and Simon Lucy. Simon was renowned for the tremendous codfish he caught almost routinely. In my year at Makkovik, I regularly held services in Inuktut for Josua and Simon, and we were sometimes joined by Johnny Akkopijok from Bob's Brook.

Josua was disabled and lived alone in a small cabin set back from the waterfront about halfway along the village pathway. Simon had no real home, but lived in quarters made for him above the Mission's carpenter shop. He and I talked for hours in Inuktut, sometimes in the mission house but more often in his room. He preferred that, though I never knew why. He was a thin, intense man, somewhat irascible. Josua, on the other hand, was happy-go-lucky and very even-tempered, as outgoing as Simon was withdrawn.

The two seemed to irritate each other and frequently quarrelled. Before I knew them well enough to see this, I suggested that they live together. It seemed clear to me that Simon, who was homeless, could be of help to Josua, who was disabled. My suggestion raised such protest and antagonism that I hastily backed off. Both men were terribly stubborn and proud of their ability to care for themselves, and each had only contempt for the other's ability as a housekeeper. Yet I could not help feeling that they enjoyed their arguments and would have found life dull without them.

The mission staff at Makkovik included myself and three teachers: Ann Pascoe, Nora Mowl and Emily Johnson, who married the Reverend Fred Grubb later that spring. In addition, the Mission employed Samuel Jacque as boatman and chapel servant and Simon, "the fish killer," as an odd job man.

That winter there were about thirty boys and girls housed in the boarding school on the ground floor of the mission house and church. Fire was a constant worry in that great wooden building full of children. The teachers relieved me of much of the work of running the school, but there always seemed to be some emergency which commanded my attention, as when Donald took to smashing windows and Pearl swallowed a hair pin. In the latter case I was quite at a loss until I remembered the trick of feeding the patient a sandwich of bread and cotton wool. Pearl ate it, reluctantly, and I suppose it helped for we had no further trouble with the child that winter.

Sam Jacque, the mission servant, was a great help in most emergencies. He was part French-Canadian and looked French, with his rather saturnine face and heavy black moustache. Sam's five o'clock shadow usually appeared about mid-morning. There was always a trickle of tobacco juice on his chin, for when he was not puffing and biting on a short-stemmed pipe he was chewing tobacco. In the winter the path from Sam's house to mine was spattered with brown spots. Sam expressed his joy in boat travel by continually singing, in a rough but somehow pleasing voice. During the winter his son, Max, was my dog team driver. We had a very pleasing relationship and shared some memorable journeys.

The final and perhaps most important member of the mission house staff was Susan Flowers, the housekeeper I had inherited from my predecessors. Susan was a very good housekeeper and an excellent cook, which enabled me to entertain parishioners and visitors in some style.

Soon after my arrival in Makkovik, a small yacht called the *Karluk* came into the harbour. It was owned by a Mr. Williams, famous for the manufacture of shaving soap and other toiletries. He was on a fishing trip along the coast and wanted to try Makkovik River the following day. I was invited to join him and his secretary, a personable young man about my own age. We left in the *Karluk* early in the morning and stopped halfway up the bay to pick up Charlie Goudie as a guide. Charlie was a brother of Jim Goudie, whose wife Elizabeth wrote the fine book, *Women of Labrador*. The result of our effort that day was a magnificent catch of salmon and char, some of which we gave to Charlie and most of the remainder to people of Makkovik.

Members of a Finnish expedition to Labrador, led by I.V. Tanner, also arrived in Makkovik that summer. I had already met some of them in Nain. The following summer Dr. Krancke of this expedition spent a great deal of time in the Makkovik-Aillik area, accompanied by a young geologist named Von Knorring. Another member of the Tanner party was a Mr. Hustich, a botanist whose work had great interest for my wife after she had joined me in Labrador and took up her own studies of the local flora. The two volume study published by the Tanner party was a magnificent work, and remains nearly half a century later the most thorough and authoritative reference on many aspects of Labrador geography.

While in Nain I had felt that the Boy Scout movement would be of great value to the local boys. I had little encouragement from my superior, but here on my own station I was free to pursue such interests. I was greatly helped by Thorwald Perrault, husband of Alice, who was the daughter of my friend and former colleague, Pa Perrett. Thorwald was at that time employed by the Hudson's Bay Company. As an outstanding woodsman he was an ideal scout leader, for he was keen to share his knowledge with the boys. I could not have had a better assistant, but our positions really should have been reversed; with his knowledge of woodcraft and survival, he should have been the scoutmaster and I his assistant.

I think, however, we were a good team, and we got all the boys and young men interested. We were lucky to have a ready-made clubhouse; a building next to the mission house which rejoiced in the name, "the white elephant." I understood that it got its name from the fact that it had been built as a dispensary with an additional room which could be used to care for patients; but it had never been used for that purpose and indeed as far as I know was never used at all until the Scouts took it over.

The Wolf Cub pack was run by Nora Mowl as cubmistress, assisted by Lavinia Andersen. We designed our own uniforms and undertook several community projects, like supplying firewood to families unable to get their own, and helping the older people get to and from church. There were also concerts, boxing exhibitions and church parades. Thorwald and his wife became so interested in scouting that when they moved to Goose Bay, where they were among the founders of the neighbouring civilian town of Happy Valley, they introduced it there as well.

Because of the size of the parish and the depth of some of the bays, my travel in the Makkovik area involved longer journeys than it had from Nain and Hopedale. On one journey into the head of Kaipokak Bay I was pursued by two of the scouts with an urgent message to return to Makkovik; a ten-year-old child was critically ill. By the time I got back, after a twenty-hour journey, the little maid had died. There was no comfort, only greater frustration, in knowing there was little I could have done for her if I had been there.

In January of that winter I was afflicted with a severe toothache. I examined my mouth as best I could and decided that one of my teeth had to come out. There was no one in the village with any knowledge of dentistry, and without someone I felt I could trust with forceps, I decided to do it myself, as incisors are not usually difficult. I had never been very good at giving a local anaesthetic and my effort this time seemed only to compound the pain, so I went ahead without it.

I took up the forceps and made one attempt, a feeble one, to remove the tooth. My courage failed me utterly and instantly. I slumped into an easy chair, cursing my cowardice and groaning with misery, then sat up with a start; the pain was gone! It was conquered, apparently, not by faith but fear. Never was there a happier coward. I had no more trouble with that tooth until it was removed by a real dentist several months later.

Some of the Makkovik trappers were accustomed to go "in country" in early October and stay till Christmas and later. One such was Uncle Charlie Goudie. He was always on the lookout for minerals while travelling in the interior and was notorious for claiming big discoveries. In the spring of 1939 he offered to cut me in on a fortune. He had discovered oil. It was dirty, thick and smelly, he said, and he had used it himself in a lamp, where it burned with a great deal of smoke. He needed two hundred dollars to outfit us to go north and stake our claim. I did not have that much, of course, and would not have staked him if I did, but I remembered the proposition when oil companies began exploratory drilling off Makkovik nearly thirty years later.

During my fourteen months in Makkovik, the people were generous in the support a young minister needed. Older members of the congregation, especially the Andersen family and Aunt Susan Mitchell, continually offered encouragement. Some helped with my studies of Inuktut.

I had left England with the understanding that I would remain in Labrador seven years before furlough. However, I had been afflicted with stomach trouble for two years. This, as well as my wish to be married and my rather obvious need for elementary medical training, convinced church authorities that I should be permitted to take furlough at the end of August, 1939. Before returning to England, I was to attend a mission conference in Nain, where the Labrador missionaries would be joined by the Reverend Estcourt Birtill, secretary to the mission board of the Moravian Church in Britain.

I was very outspoken at this conference, expressing my alarm at the social and economic state of the Labrador people. After one heated session Brother Birtill called me aside. Expecting a reprimand, I was startled to get a promotion instead. Reverend Paul Hettasch, the superintendent of the Mission, was to retire in Germany in June, 1941. After my furlough, I was to return as his assistant for a year, then take over his position when he left. This was a shock, since there were three brethren older than myself, with many more years of service in Labrador.

On the last day of our week-long meetings, we heard that war was declared between Britain and Germany. It fell to Paul Hettasch to announce this to the settlers and Inuit gathered in Nain. I felt a deep compassion for this man and his wife who were now suddenly enemy aliens in a land to which they had given almost fifty years of service. Clearly they could not return to Germany now. Neither ever saw their fatherland again, and both died in the United States.

At the end of the conference I returned to Makkovik and packed my bags for England. How and when I would get there was not clear, given the uncertainties of shipping and war. I had no difficulty reaching St. John's, where Job Brothers had reserved a room at the Newfoundland Hotel. They had also booked my passage on the next Furness–Withy ship to Liverpool, but no one knew when or even if it would reach St. John's, because German U-boats were already haunting the North Atlantic.

For two weeks I kicked my heels around St. John's, visited friends and did a great deal of thinking about my work in Labrador. With a bit of respite and some distance, I could be more objective about the problems of Inuit and settlers. It was obvious to me that they were fighting a losing battle against poverty and disease, and that unless changes were made the Inuit would be extinct before many more years had passed. The situation of the Indians was even worse.

People of northern Labrador, a thousand miles from the capital of a territory which was itself a struggling colony of Britain, were out of sight and out of mind. I felt that when I became superintendent of the Mission one of my tasks must be to make the government of Newfoundland more aware of its northern citizens. Above all, they needed better medical service. The medical work of missionaries and one or two visits a year from Grenfell Mission doctors was just not enough.

It also seemed to me that there was too much "empire building" in Labrador and that the Mission's mandate to keep undesirable influences at bay, an authority which went back to the origins of the Moravian Church in Labrador, could be easily abused. I resolved that whatever the temptation I would not promote my own interests at the expense of the people I had come to serve. It was clear to me that all of us, Inuit, settlers and outsiders, needed each other's skills and experience, and that harmony grew from this interdependence.

While these thoughts crowded my mind, I was also much exercised about when and how I would reach England and Doris, whom I had not seen for more than four years. Then came cautious word that the S.S. *Newfoundland* would leave St. John's on the first of October. This was very hush-hush, though the ship was now in port and it must have been widely known that she was bound for Liverpool. We boarded on the night of 30 September and sailed without escort the next morning.

Two days later we reached Halifax, where more passengers joined us. We were attached to a convoy which our ship would lead. In darkness our twenty-odd vessels slipped out of Halifax harbour, grey ships under grey skies, crawling, it seemed, through grey seas. We shuddered at thoughts of submarines, cruising like vast grey sharks in search of prey.

Our passengers included a few English returning after holidays in Canada or the U.S., a handful of students returning to Oxford and Cambridge, and a senior postal official who had been working in St. John's with the Commission of Government. There was a Newfoundlander who was a flying officer in the Royal Air Force, recalled to his unit. Angus Fridge, the Hudson's Bay Company factor from Davis Inlet, was dashing home to enlist. So was Roy Hammond, who had been working for Richard White at Kauk Harbour. There was a collection of others whose reasons for travelling to England seemed obscure.

The officers and passengers, including Admiral Tizzard, the commander of the convoy, became a close-knit community in the days that followed. We made painfully slow progress. Since this was one of the first convoys of the war the ships, like our passengers, were a motley collection. None of them had much speed, and of course the slowest vessel set the pace. Our crossing took twenty-one nervous days.

One of the students returning to Oxford was Henry Hicks, coxswain of the Oxford boat crew for 1939. Later he became premier of Nova Scotia, then president of Dalhousie University and finally a senator. Henry was soon organizing life on board. He decided that the ship was to be my parish while the voyage lasted, and formed a choir to sing at church services held in the ship's lounge every Sunday. He and several of us produced a ship's newspaper.

Our days were full of a false gaiety, beneath which lurked a good deal of apprehension. This was especially so when we were abandoned by our escort five hundred miles out from Halifax. On one occasion, as we moved darkly over the sea with not a glimmer of light showing from the convoy, an American ship with all her lights ablaze steamed right through our midst, provoking much annoyance.

Somewhere in mid-Atlantic there was a call to lifeboat stations in the middle of the night. It was a false alarm, though passengers didn't know it. Had it been a real emergency I might well have gone down with the ship, for instead of going immediately to my boat station I packed a small case and then shaved! I cannot imagine why. When I finally started out for the boat deck everyone else was coming back, or almost everyone. Angus Fridge had slept through it all.

One morning we were much relieved to discover that we had been joined in the night by two destroyers, which now herded our convoy about like a couple of motherly sheep dogs. Occasionally, too, a surveillance aircraft would appear. This added to our sense of security, though in fact we were now entering the period of greatest danger.

One Sunday near the end of the voyage we were having our religious service in the lounge, thanking Almighty God for bringing us safely across the ocean, when one of Admiral Tizzard's staff appeared at the door. He made a signal to the admiral, who rose quickly and left. We learned later that a U-boat had been spotted in our vicinity and our destroyers pursued it. On 24 October, a full three weeks out of Halifax, we docked in Liverpool. Christopher Columbus, sighting the New World and thinking it China, could not have been happier.

Wartime Britain was not yet a very different place than the country I had left, though blackouts and rationing were soon to make themselves felt.

Arriving in Bristol, where my mother still lived, I was met by my family and fiancée. We promptly made plans to marry 30 December. I was supposed to seek permission of the church to marry, but I was in no mood for technicalities. The Church Board had been evacuated from London to Tytherton, in Wiltshire, and I met them there to confirm my appointment as superintendent and make plans for the future. Among other things we arranged that Doris and I would take a short course at the Missionary School of Medicine in Great Ormond Street, London. Our studies would commence in the first week of January, and we would sail for Newfoundland in July.

In the meantime, I must see to my stomach. Visits to assorted doctors and specialists did me no good, but certainly no harm. They attributed my problem to an ulcer, to imagination, to nerves and even to lovesickness, but they told me nothing very certain or convincing. However, I found my health improving as our wedding date approached.

We were married in Maudlin Street Moravian Church, Bristol, close to the spot from which John Cabot sailed to discover Newfoundland. We spent a few days honeymoon at a place called Latimer Lodge in the Royal forest of Dean, before leaving again for London. There we boarded with a woman who was cook at the missionary school's residence for singles. Her husband Harold was a London bus driver.

Although courses at the school were intended for missionaries going to the tropics, we found much that was helpful and interesting. In addition to lectures we were allowed to attend clinics, watch operations and do ward rounds in hospitals of the area. The course was a satisfying experience, and gave me more confidence in my medical role in Labrador. We both passed with high marks.

Doris pleaded for a course in midwifery, which we knew would be invaluable in our work. Eventually she was allowed to get some experience at a hospital in the east end of London. The first day she witnessed a caesarian section, which was interesting but not useful. However, she was excited that her course had begun. That was on a Friday. By Sunday, she was covered with the spots of German measles, and any further study of midwifery was abandoned.

It was a bitterly cold winter that year; the Thames actually froze. We felt the cold particularly on weekends, when I was asked to preach in different churches about the work of the Mission in Labrador. The houses we stayed in on these jaunts were almost invariably large and frigid in proportion to the warmth of the hospitality we enjoyed. The bedrooms seemed not to have been occupied since the last missionary visited.

After a short holiday, we made final preparations for our departure. In this period, "the phony war" ended and the real one began. The Maginot Line was smashed. We stood on the sidewalk in a throng of thousands and cheered the troops returning from Dunkirk. These tattered, weaponless and in some cases bootless men were received like conquering heroes, not an army which had barely escaped annihilation. The uncertain period of waiting was now replaced by determination. The nation gritted its teeth, rallied by the magnificent leadership of Churchill, who made several of his most memorable speeches in this period.

While staying with my mother in Bristol we experienced a number of air raids, mostly at night, but the blitz had not really begun and damage was slight. A year later, much of the centre of Bristol was devastated.

Although we knew we would return to Labrador early in July, the details of our departure were kept extremely vague. Suddenly we were instructed to send our freight to a certain pier in Liverpool. We did, and that was the last we saw of most of it. Just as suddenly we were told to report to another pier in the same city. Arriving there with nothing more than our hand luggage and a letter from the Mission Board to the Furness-Withy agent, we were very thoroughly searched and interrogated. Then, limp with weariness and frustration, we were left alone and allowed to just sit and wait.

At last we were conducted aboard the S.S. *Nerissa*, a ship of the Bermuda run of the Furness-Withy line. A most unpleasant smell, like that of rotting turnips, permeated the vessel. There were hundreds of passengers, including the crews of several ships torpedoed earlier on the voyage we were about to make. We remained in port the rest of that day and night, then joined a convoy just before dawn.

Just outside the mouth of the Mersey we sailed passed the wreckage of ships caught in the jaws of war and beached in the shallows. An even more chilling sight were the gaping holes in the hulls of an incoming convoy. It seemed obvious that the war was going badly. My passage to England the previous fall had been a gala party compared to the sense of doom which now settled over the *Nerissa*. However, convoys were now composed of ships of like speed so that we made better time, despite one attack on our convoy. Within eleven days we could smell the spruce forests of Nova Scotia as we crept through fog into Halifax harbour.

After a day in Halifax, our ship made a solo dash for St. John's, which took three days. There, we learned that we would sail on the *Kyle* to Hopedale and on the *Winnifred Lee* to Nain. Here in Newfoundland the war seemed like a remote fantasy, and our journey along the coast of Newfoundland and Labrador was a restful treat after the tension of the broad Atlantic. Doris, who had majored in botany at Cardiff, now took to jigging fish at every harbour. The harvest was chiefly sculpins.

As she wrote in a letter to her parents:

> "By tonight we should have reached Hopedale and then we have a day's journey in a schooner before arriving in Nain . . . . We called at all the little fishing harbours on the Coast of Newfoundland. The whole village turned out on the wharf at every port of call . . . . The first real excitement came when we sighted an iceberg away on the horizon. It looked rather like an island in the distance. Soon others followed and we passed much nearer to them — strange, weird shapes which seemed scarcely to be moving. In the sunshine the rounded, wave-worn surfaces glistened as if they had been polished and the shadows were beautiful pale blue-green. This morning I counted twenty-five icebergs around the ship and they have made the weather very cold. Several days have been so warm that one has had to seek the shade on the deck. At Battle Harbour there was one enormous iceberg aground and while we were there we saw it breaking up. Tons and tons of ice fell into the sea with an enormous splash.
>
> Yesterday at Cartwright the first real Eskimo woman came aboard. She had been in the hospital and is on her way north to Hopedale. She and Bill have been carrying on a conversation in Eskimo. I can understand a few of the words and that gives me at least an idea of the drift of the conversation. She is a short, yellow-skinned, flat-faced, narrow-eyed little woman with straight black hair and very dark eyes.
>
> . . . . When we get to harbour, and sometimes out at sea, hosts of little fishing boats come around half filled with codfish and herring (still kicking) and the fishermen want to receive their mail . . . .
> The coast is very bleak and rugged, but sometimes we go for long runs up tickles, between the islands and the mainland, and this is just grand. The air is warmer, the country more interesting. The most beautiful places are up the inlets where the water just mirrors the sky and the spruce-covered hills which rise steeply from the water's edge. We were up such an inlet last night when the sun was setting and I cannot describe the beauty of colour and reflection. Pale blue mountains in the distance were covered with snow. As we came down the inlet the moon was shining across the water and the mackerel sky was an absolute picture.

My disappointment at not seeing more wildlife in the Atlantic has been well compensated. I have seen several schools of porpoises and several grampuses. The latter are like small whales. Outside of some of the harbours the huskies are left on the islands for the summer.

There is lots more I could tell you but I am missing all there is to be seen on deck."

We landed in Hopedale, 11 August, where we waited a day before boarding the *Winnifred Lee*. She was no ordinary schooner. She was 110 feet long with a draught of 12 feet and a gross burden of 149 tons. She was built in Shelburne, Nova Scotia, as a banker, then converted for use as a coastal schooner. When purchased by the family of Captain Joshua Winsor, she was refitted with a diesel engine, then used as a mail boat and freighter along the coast from Hopedale to Hebron. She boasted a large cabin aft, roomy enough for six double bunks. One of these was for the captain, the remainder for passengers. The crew of six slept forward in the galley and dining area.

Our voyage north from Hopedale was slow but fascinating, for it was the role of the *Winnifred Lee* to carry mail and news to the Newfoundland fishing schooners in the area as well as to the coastal villages. Only a few of the schooners had radio transmitters but they all had receivers and used these to keep informed of the progress of our boat. Doris fished at every stop and began to do well at it. She also spent a great deal of time peeling potatoes, which endeared her to the cook. She found everything exciting: the restless sea, the increasing magnificence of the scenery, the warmth of the people we met and the sunny days of our voyage; it could not have been better.

Then in Drawbucket Tickle, a few hours from Nain, fog blotted out everything around us. In those pre-radar days there was nothing to be done but sit it out, and we sat for three days. At last the dense pall lifted and in brilliant sunshine we steamed into our new home, Nain.

9

HOME IN NAIN

My life now took on an entirely new dimension. I had been oppressed by a terrible loneliness during my first four years in Labrador. Separated from the woman I loved, there wasn't anyone with whom I could share my hopes and ideas. Now I was to enter a period when our physical isolation was not isolation at all, but an opportunity to commune with nature and each other without the distractions of life in cities. In this and later chapters I will quote extensively from Doris's letters, which express the delight and at times the shock of her first few years in Nain.

I have always maintained that isolation is more a state of mind than geography. Our only real hardship was our worry about our families in war-battered England, for we heard from them quite infrequently. Even in summer, we were lucky to get mail more than every two weeks; in winter we had just three deliveries from October to June. However, it was possible, even in the dark days of war, to get news of friends and family through the "Northern Messenger" service of the Canadian Broadcasting Corporation (CBC). This weekly programme, broadcast all across the Arctic and sub-Arctic, relayed messages of twenty-five words or less to residents of remote communities. It was an excellent service, a joy to its audience.

The announcers fixed the order of the messages by taking names in alphabetical order one week, and in the reverse order the next. Because "P" is roughly in the middle of the alphabet, we listened faithfully every week and found ourselves peeking in on the lives of people all over the north. The entire audience became a kind of fellowship, almost as familiar with the details of each other's lives as residents of a small town. We wondered how Constable Pearce in Baffin Land, who got messages from half a dozen women around the country, would handle this problem when he went on furlough. Later we learned (through the Northern Messenger) that the girl he married was someone else again.

Though most of the audience for this show were outsiders, Inuit with relatives in southern hospitals also enjoyed the service. I know that many of the Inuit of Nain were listeners, for they often greeted us the morning after the show with comments about messages we had received.

There was much wrong with our house in Nain, but it was a palace compared to most. However, during my absence from Nain another missionary, a bachelor and keen photographer, had occupied the house. He had used the galvanized iron kitchen sink to develop and fix his photographs. Gradually the chemicals had eaten dozens of tiny holes in the metal, so that it sprayed like a shower when Doris went to use it. She went immediately to Reverend Hettasch and asked for another. He looked at her in horror. "Don't you know there's a war on?"

A short time later an old Inuk appeared with a soldering iron, solder and paste. Slowly, patiently and methodically he covered every tiny hole with a blob of solder, until our sink had more warts than a toad. "*Tava*," he announced proudly. "That's it." Until I was able to buy a new sink the following year, Doris had to use the old one with the utmost care to avoid dislodging the little blobs of solder.

We were determined that in spite of the difficulties and worries of our work—the sickness and poverty, inadequate education and hygiene, and the appalling infant mortality, especially in Hebron— we would take joy in each other and in the experiences we could share. My wife, who was as clever as she was beautiful, was a scientist able to help me appreciate life in the north far more than I could when I was *Angutainak*, the man alone. Excerpts from one of her first letters home convey her excitement:

> The most exciting time in the fall was when the sea froze over. For weeks before, the brook at the end of the bay had frozen and broken up continually and great pieces of ice were being carried out to sea on the tide. For several days the sea was covered with soft, slushy, "slob ice" which went out on the tide, although the boulders and all the supports of the wharf were covered with a thick layer of ice and the crossbars were hanging with enormous icicles. The shore was frozen and the margin of the sea was covered with ice, and then in a single night the bay froze and never broke up again.

The very next day men were out at the edge of the ice—sitting about a mile away from the shore—waiting for seals. As soon as the ice was firm it started to blow, a bitterly cold, penetrating wind that froze the face. The snow drifted until travelling became impossible and the seal hunt was a failure. A few seals were caught in nets but the number was very small compared with former years and as a result the people have no meat for themselves and their dogs—no boot skins and no skins for trading. I don't think they could ever have been so poor. The best time for hunting seals is when there are still open places in the ice, due to currents and tide, and you can well imagine that such places are dangerous in bad weather.

It gave me a great thrill to see the first *komatik* and dogs, but the finest sight was at Christmas time when I saw half a dozen *komatiks* all at once on the sea ice. The sea ice is not smooth and shiny, but the surface is covered with a thick layer of snow and salt which has been whipped up by the wind so that it resembles wave-marked sand. Walking is comparatively easy if there is little soft snow. Bill would not let me go on the ice before Christmas, but the Sunday before last was a lovely day and we walked right across the bay. The most difficult part is near the shore where the rise and fall of the tide has heaped the ice into enormous masses and one is almost reduced to crawling over the great fissures . . .

Christmas was about the most hectic time I have ever had in my life. We decorated our living room and had a lovely Christmas tree and all looked very festive . . . . We went out visiting the Eskimo houses in the afternoon and everybody had a Christmas tree and lit all the candles for us to see. It amazed me to see the variety of decoration. Even the sweets and biscuits which the children had received the day before were hung with cotton on the tree and beneath were the children's gifts. In church there were two big Christmas trees decorated with candles and a third tree was brought in on Christmas Eve, decorated with presents for all the children up to fourteen years of age. We had all spent several nights the previous week making and mending toys and packing candy. The gifts were distributed after the carol service. That was a lovely service held entirely by candle light. The Christmas tree was fitted into a stand which was wound up and rotated, turning the tree around gradually as it played a tune like a musical box. Every seat in the church was occupied as it was throughout the whole of Christmas.

When we were not in church with the people, they were with us at home. For at least a couple of hours on Christmas night there were forty people in our dining room, but they were enjoying themselves. We gave them sweets, biscuits and cigarettes and we kept them occupied with picture books and the gramophone. The din was terrific! I don't think you can imagine what a hullabaloo it was . . . .

It was about Wednesday of the next week before we managed to get away. I filled the big thermos with hot soup and the small one with cocoa. We took some chocolate and two hunks of hard bread, packed it in the haversack and left Nain. There had been little snow for weeks and the paths were more smooth and level than a London pavement, and decidedly cleaner.

We walked through the woods until we came to the frozen brook. Unlike the sea ice the fresh water ice is very slippery unless it is snow-covered, and we had the greatest difficulty in walking. Instead of being absolutely level the ice on the brook was pushed up into great bulges by the pressure of the water below. This water bursts out every so often . . . .

Soon, as we went upward, the brook was covered in snow—packed hard and smooth like a paved road by the *komatiks* which almost always follow this path when the men are wooding. First we came to a small pond, frozen solid, and then to a huge lake. Here in places the ice had been blown clean of snow and was black and clear except for little white bubbles, and a few cracks which you could see stretching downwards at least a yard through the clear ice. This lake is a very deep one and is called the "Trouser Leg," presumably because it forks into two long arms like a pair of trousers. It was a horrible sensation to look down into the blackness. At the edge of this pond we lunched and watched the first of the *komatiks*, and dogs going home after a morning's wooding.

There are plenty of trees just behind the station, chiefly spruce and larch with an undergrowth of willow and alder, but the bigger trees have all been cut out higher up the brook. It is only when one gets to the Trouser Leg that the bigger trees start to appear once more.

Going inland from the Trouser Leg we crossed a third lake and eventually reached a fourth. The land was gradually getting grander as the trees grew taller and the hills were higher. It reminded me more of the pictures one sees of the Canadian Rockies with the snow-clad mountains, the black fir trees and the still lakes. If it were not so cold without gloves I might try to paint it for you, but the water would freeze solid before we had half got there, and the brush would freeze before one could get the water on the paper.

My young wife's interest in the plants and birds of the north opened up an entirely new life for me. We wandered through the woods and over hills the next summer and the next, searching out rare plants and flowers, spotting elusive song birds. We travelled by boat to some of the more remote bays and the outside fishing places, and it seemed that in each place Doris was able to show me some exciting new facet of our environment.

Life was idyllic, and our northland home became more fascinating day by day. My health was still poor; I had continual attacks of vomiting, but I was determined not to let it spoil things for us. Doris worried, but kept her worry to herself.

We both had much to learn. Although she was an excellent cook and housekeeper, Doris was now faced with foods and domestic problems she had never met before. To begin with, the Bay stocked only the bare staples; you didn't dash down for a loaf of bread or some pork chops. In fact, we did our shopping once a year, by mail. It was sometimes possible to get a supplementary order in mid-summer, but that took at least six weeks and we never found the St. John's merchants very speedy about filling orders for Labrador.

There had been a time when all the Mission's and the missionaries' supplies were purchased wholesale in England and admitted into Newfoundland duty-free. This compensated in some measure for our low salaries. But with the coming of war we had to order provisions through St. John's at much higher prices, so that it took great ingenuity to get by on a missionary's salary.

Sometimes, of course, buying food at a distance led to absurd mistakes. Once when we had ordered a case of forty-eight fourteen ounce tins of grapefruit we got a case of twelve seven-pound tins instead. The tins were so battered that every one leaked. We were heartily sick of grapefruit before it was gone.

Doris adapted superbly to the demands of her new environment. She was soon able to clean fish with the best of them and to face without blanching the delivery of a porcupine carcass or the haunch of a caribou or bear. The Inuit always came to sell us a bit of whatever fresh meat or birds they had, and after a time we found we could eat nearly every meat that came our way, shunning only ravens and foxes. Doris wrote in January, 1941:

> This winter has, so far, not been particularly good for fresh meat. I have been very careful with what we have and we are managing quite well so far. There are very few partridges compared with last year, I am told. At the moment I have seven white ones, an Arctic hare and a duck—all frozen. We have not had deer (caribou) meat since the fall, but Bill never seems to get tired of partridge. There are three kinds of partridge—two white and one greyish-brown. The smaller white ones live up on the barrens and the larger ones are found in the brooks. The grey ones live in the woods and feed on spruce leaves while the white ones live on willow buds. You can actually taste spruce in the grey ones and it is not at all unpleasant.

The mission had a large garden which we shared with our colleagues. Earlier generations of missionaries had carted soil from the woodlands and made a garden on a southerly slope. Over many years they had carefully worked out the tricks of gardening in this place, and Uncle Paul Hettasch initiated us into this lore. Before he left Nain, he handed us a beautifully-written gardening calendar which served us well for many years.

The growing season was short, but the days in that brief season were long and bright. In June, plants could grow twenty hours a day. We started seeds in shallow trays in the kitchen window in late March or April, then transplanted them into hot beds in May. Here the seedlings of lettuce, cabbage, kholrabi and even cauliflower could make a good beginning, before we moved them at last to the open ground. We sowed carrots and beets in the open, hopefully before the last snowfall. The business of thinning them later was a painful contest between the gardener and the mosquitos. We grew cabbage and lettuce in the hot beds for early salads, and cauliflower and more cabbage for winter storage. Rhubarb, originally imported from Europe, grew profusely and supplied everyone around, including the crews of visiting ships.

Doris even tried to grow cucumbers, which would have been a coup if she had done it. She lovingly nursed the seedlings in the house and set them out in frames when the weather was warm enough, taking the usual precautions against the raids of mice. Nevertheless the tender plants were gone next morning. Nothing remained but small moist spots in the soil and tiny paw prints leading from a hole in one corner of the frame. Doris was furious, and set out poisoned peas. Revenge was not sweet, exactly, but it was swift and certain; we harvested a great number of dead mice. Later a subtle, unpleasant smell seeped through my study, until I had to crawl under the house to find the source. Once again: dead mice.

Our garden crop was usually rich but some years, when Arctic ice lingered on the coast and chilled the summer air, the harvest was pathetic. After weeks of long hours in the garden, this could be heartbreaking. We often went out at six in the morning and got in several hours of weeding and hoeing before our other work began. We also spent many hours watering until we devised an irrigation system. Often the huskies played havoc in the garden, for the fence and gates were in poor condition. The lintel on the western gate was carved with the year the garden was begun—1832. In all this time few repairs had been done to the fences, so we had our hands full. Missionaries who followed us at Nain found the upkeep of the garden too laborious and gave it up.

Toward the end of summer there were several species of berries to harvest, preserve and store for winter. One time, wandering along the shore, we came across a large patch of red berries. I took them for partridgeberries—a form of cranberry—and assured Doris they were both safe and delicious. We picked enough for a pie, and ate the pie but found it tasteless. The following day Doris spoke of this to Tante Hettasch, who insisted firmly that partridgeberries would still be pale and unripe; this must be something else. Further investigation revealed that we had eaten bear berries, alleged to be indigestible and even poisonous. I can report that the only damage in this case was to my ego.

The last idyllic days of our first summer together in Nain passed all too quickly. With the coming of the fall equinox, the winds and sudden storms made small boat travel perilous but the Inuit carried on hunting and fishing, coming to the station only for supplies, medical aid and sometimes for Sunday services. By this time most of the Newfoundland schooners had long gone south and we were waiting for the final trip of the *Winnifred Lee*.

One very stormy afternoon I was working in my study when the Newfoundland Ranger, Dean Bragg, came in with the news that a trap boat was in trouble off Nain Point. He wanted the use of the Mission launch, the *Seeko*, to attempt a rescue. So off we went with several Inuit, including Dick Pamak, an extremely strong and capable man who later became a special constable in the RCMP. Nain is a poor harbour and we had great difficulty making our way through heavy seas toward the boat, which had lost its engine and was drifting to destruction on the ugly rocks off the point. Dean steered the *Seeko* while I tried to coax our rather ancient engine to better effort.

Eventually we were able to get a line aboard the drifting trap boat, thanks to the seamanship of Dean and Dick. Now our problem was to bring our five-ton vessel and the trap boat back to safety through heavy seas. We had to cross the harbour and steam in under the lee of Nain Hill. People watching from shore feared time and again that we would be swamped. Altogether the rescue took three hours, and throughout this time I dreaded engine failure, for the old Gray engine in the *Seeko* was on its last legs and I was a poor mechanic.

This incident was one of many challenges which drove home to me both my own limitations and the versatility of my neighbours.

Like other homes in the village in those days, ours was heated by wood stoves, though we had the tall, Dutch, tiled stoves which kept their heat much longer than the iron stoves and kitchen ranges common in the rest of the village. These Dutch stoves were five to six feet tall, a yard deep and two feet wide. They were easy to regulate, but tended to build up soot. We lived with the fear that a chimney fire would get out of control and destroy the house.

The last chore of each day was to make shavings and splits (kindling) to start the fires in the morning. When the stoves went out at night, the house could get desperately cold when the temperature dropped to minus twenty Farenheit and winter gales howled around us.

We had running water in the summer, but had to disconnect and drain the system in October. The pipes, which were of wood, ran from a small dam to the mission house and a public fountain from which the villagers drew their water in summer. The pipes were six-foot logs bored with a three-foot auger owned by the mission and imported especially for that purpose. It was kept at the home of Amos Voisey, who for years had the delicate job of boring pipes and keeping the system supplied with replacements. In winter, everyone had to haul water by dog sled from the dam, or from the brook which empties into the head of the bay.

Doris described the complications of her first winter in a letter to her parents, January 14, 1941:

> Winter started almost immediately. The *Fort Garry*, the Hudson's Bay Company mail boat, went south in October — in fact she was held up in the next inlet by a terrific snowstorm which lasted three days. Since then there has constantly been snow on the ground, although this winter the snow has been light until this weekend. I have only been outside the door but the front of the house is almost buried in drifts at least twelve feet high. The lower panes of the dining room windows are blocked up and if it were possible to open the window we could take a beautifully long slide down toward the church at an angle of about forty-five degrees. The temperature was exceptionally low all the fall and I have had my work cut out to prevent things from freezing in the "warm store room". . . .

> Water is rather a problem now. I have one big tank in the kitchen and another in the passage. The ice on the latter is about three inches thick and Bill breaks it with a hammer or mallet every morning. The kitchen tank has to be refilled about once a week and we have to get two men to do it. They take a sledge, with two barrels lashed on, to the water hole — about a quarter of a mile away. The water hole is about a foot in diameter and is situated over

a deep part of the stream which flows into the brook. The ice is about a foot thick. The buckets are lowered through the hole and the barrels are filled and brought back to the house. The tank is filled through a pipe in the wall from a box outside. The buckets, barrels, box and pipe get covered with a thick coating of ice and I have to poke a stick along the pipe to keep it open . . . .

Washing is another problem. The clothes freeze in your hands before you get them on the line so I usually dry things indoors. Bill has fixed me up a half dozen strong lines in the kitchen and everything is usually dry by Monday night.

Once a week or once a fortnight we get a man to fill up the woodshed with some dry and some green wood and then we have a stack brought into each room in the morning and piled behind the stove. When it is very windy the wood just disappears like fun.

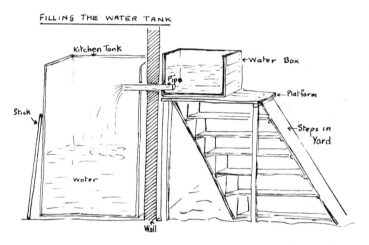

FILLING THE WATER TANK

Doris had originally planned to be a missionary in Africa. During our early years in Labrador I often felt guilty when I saw her looking pinched and cold; I wondered if she ever regretted her marriage and pined for the warmth of Africa. At any rate, she never complained. As the years passed, we got better at coping with our environment and found a certain exuberance in the challenges it posed. We had great times together shovelling the immense masses of snow which always seemed to be gathering on our front steps and against the lower windows. I should admit, though, that often our Inuit neighbours were already digging us out by the time we got started.

In that first year, I was gradually taking over the operation of both the Nain station and the mission field from Paul Hettasch. The mission was financed from England; apart from a few thousand dollars in a discretionary account in St. John's, all expenses were handled from London. Job Brothers and the Hudson's Bay Company were our agents and suppliers. The missionaries handled small amounts of petty cash but nothing more, not even their salaries. The London office paid the missionaries' accounts once a year and sent them an annual statement. It was a system prone to great confusion and discontent. In addition, the extreme poverty of our Inuit congregation made demands on the missionaries' personal resources, and none of us really knew how we stood financially at any given time.

Apart from the business of the mission, I was to supervise the religious work of our missionaries, and to arbitrate any disputes that arose. This meant that in addition to running my own station and visiting the settlers and Inuit in my district, I had to visit the other missions at least twice a year. This entailed a dog team trip of about 750 miles, which would take at least a month, and a boat trip of about the same length which took two weeks. After years of this I welcomed the coming of aircraft.

Having been frustrated in her midwifery by measles, Doris was still determined to get some training. She apprenticed herself to an Inuit lady named Kristiana Sillitt, wife of Gustav, whose reputation in this was extremely high. In turn, Doris taught Kristiana how to preserve meat and other foods in bottles.

This was the pattern of life in Nain. It seemed that all of us, Inuit, settlers and "outsiders", were continually learning from each other to the enrichment of all. The storekeeeper Jim Delaney, and his assistant Duncan, the Newfoundland Ranger Dean Bragg and his wife Nora, Paul and Helen Hettasch and the teachers, Kate Hettasch and Polly Shaw, were the other outsiders. While we did not always agree, we did have a sense of community often lacking in such settlements.

Jim Delaney was a compassionate Newfoundlander and a friend to the native population. He also had a great sense of humour and an ability to laugh at himself, a very necessary quality for those who would live in the north. He did not leave Nain when the Hudson's Bay Company pulled out in 1942, but was loaned to the Newfoundland Government for a year. Leaving Nain in 1943, travelling to a Company post in southern Labrador, he fell dead beside his dog team. His death was a great loss to the Company and to Labrador.

The whites in our community were not addicted to alcohol, and there was little drinking anywhere in the village in those years. Among the Inuit there were occasional drinking bouts on home brew, which could be made from many things, apparently, but molasses was the most common ingredient. Sometimes hardtack was used as well. The results were nearly always potent and noxious.

The authorities overlooked quiet drinking, but if home brew led to commotion or quarrels the missionary or the Ranger would go to the house, confiscate the brew and pour it out. Usually within a few days the offenders would present themselves at the office and express their regrets. Occasionally Rangers would press charges and send samples of the brew out for analysis of its alcohol content. The brew was often still working, so that by the time it reached St. John's the alcohol content was high. Offenders brought before the magistrate were usually fined a few dollars and that was the end of it. There was none of the constant drunkenness and violence common in many northern communities today.

While it is true that more alcohol is available today, I believe it is also true that winter idleness is one of the chief causes of Inuit alcoholism. A wave of profound changes, some for the better, some worse, has overtaken the culture we came to know in Nain in the mid-thirties. Gone are many of the traditional pursuits which kept people active and scattered along the coast in small camps much of the year. Today they congregate in crowded homes in a crowded village, leading a life which is alien to their spirit and foreign to their culture.

Until the 1960s the Inuit and Indians were not permitted to drink, which was, of course, discrimination. Enforcement was complicated by the failure of the law to define Inuk or Indian. In the absence of a definition, arbitrary distinctions prevailed. Thus the formal opinion of the justice department, given to me personally in 1940, was that an Inuk was anyone whose father was an Inuk, regardless of the race of the mother. The child of an Inuit mother by a white father was legally white, yet the child of a white woman by an Inuit father was legally Inuit. If a woman had children by two husbands, one white and one Inuit, some would be Inuit and some would not. Presumably the same peculiar logic governed the definition of Indians.

Another problem with the administration of justice in the north was the long delay. If "justice delayed is justice denied," then we got little justice; the magistrate usually came once a year. An Inuk charged with some trivial offence might not be brought before the magistrate for more than a year after his offence was committed. Often he had forgotten all about it and did not know why he was being prosecuted. In any case, since the Inuit are forgiving people, he saw no reason why he should not be forgiven after so long. Often the police were equally frustrated by these delays, which made it difficult to instil any respect for the legal system they were trying to uphold; they felt the justice department was letting them down. The magistrates, on the whole, were understanding men who had sympathy with the Inuit, although there were cases of harsh punishment.

In our little northern Labrador communities the death of one individual and the sorrow of the immediate mourners affected the whole village. While we were in some ways divided into three groups, we were united in times of crisis, sorrow, worship or joy.

In early June, 1941, we were all saddened by the death of Nora (Mowl) Bragg, who died giving birth to a stillborn child. Her difficult labour was the occasion of the first mercy flight into northern Labrador. Jim Delaney, the storekeeper, was also the radio operator. When it became obvious that the birth would be difficult, Jim tried to reach the Grenfell Mission at Cartwright. In those days there were no planes on the coast and the base in Goose Bay was not yet established. By some miracle a plane *en route* to England heard the frantic messages from the tiny transmitter in Nain. The plane diverted to Cartwright, picked up Dr. Forsyth and flew him to Nain. He arrived too late.

This tragedy made me more determined than ever to work for a better medical service. That summer I made my first overtures to the Commission of Government to provide a cottage hospital and a nurse for Nain. Twelve years would pass before we got them.

I have already described how central was the role of the missionary in the education, health, religious life and general well-being of our community, and how that authority was shared with the council of elders, or *AngajoKauKattiget*. The duties of the elders were clear and well understood until the 1960s, when some bureaucrat who knew nothing of the form of self-government already in place decided that northern Labrador communities needed village councils. The result was needless duplication and confusion, with the government-sponsored council demanding control over many local affairs formerly governed by the elders, and expecting the elders to confine themselves to fund-raising events. Had government seen fit to consult local people and the Mission, the only institution which had really cared for the Inuit over a period of nearly two hundred years, this would have been avoided.

Such bungling has formed a consistent pattern in government dealing with our native people in this province and indeed in Canada generally, in the past. Decisions are far too often made in the absence of feedback from those most affected, by officials who presume to know better. One of the most bizarre examples occured in 1948, when someone in the Department of Natural Resources in the Commission of Government conceived the plan of moving the Indians of Davis Inlet to Okak, 160 miles north. This was an environment so alien to the Indians that in the dead of winter in 1949, facing starvation and death, they walked back to Davis Inlet. Shortly after this event the Roman Catholic church provided a resident priest, who could intercede on their behalf and prevent such folly in future.

Ledum groenlandicum

Labrador Tea

10

THINGS MEDICAL

Taking responsibility for the health of some four hundred people along 150 miles of coast, as I did when I first landed in Hopedale, was no small task for one whose medical training was the first aid learned in Boy Scouts sixteen years before. Patients sometimes died, of course, leaving me to wonder if they died in spite of my desperate effort or because of it. All the other missionaries on the north coast had received some medical training at Livingstone College in London. I had not, because of the urgency of my call to Labrador. I applied myself as best I could, reading avidly from the few medical books on hand. Later I acquired a new Merck manual, an aid to diagnosis and treatment, which was a great help.

My lack of preparation was especially serious in that I arrived in Labrador at a time of crisis. The Depression, cruel everywhere, was compounded in northern Labrador by a shortage of the game on which people still heavily depended. Sealing and caribou hunting failed year after year. Poverty was extreme. Stores stocked minimal supplies and "poor relief" was not enough to keep anyone healthy.

Many of the Inuit and some settlers lived in one-room shacks. In these homes pain, disease and death strutted across the hearth. Hunger produced pot-bellied children raised with little hope of health, often condemned to an early death by tuberculosis or meningitis.

Storekeepers and some missionaries claimed that Indians and Inuit could not live on a white man's diet. It was clear to me that what afflicted them was a totally inadequate white man's diet, consisting largely of white bread, margarine and tea sweetened with molasses. This could scarcely nourish a pregnant woman or sustain a hunter whose work called for heavy and sustained effort, sometimes in extreme cold.

Naturally, the Inuit sometimes treated their own ills. By my time, some of their traditional remedies had given way to modern medicine, while others lingered on. Some are still current today.

They gave a stew of willow bark to those who spit up or coughed blood, though this remedy seems not to have been used much after about 1940. I failed to discover dosage. They used the root of sedum, a rosette-like plant very common on the coast, as a painkiller. They also ate the buds of willow, with a dressing of molasses, as a salad and a preventive of scurvy. They used the spores of the puff ball (*Lycoperdon gemmatum*) directly on cuts and wounds. Many still use juniper sap for cuts, and swear by its healing properties.

They treated influenza with Labrador Tea (*Ledum grroenlandicum*), an infusion of which they drank half a cup at a time to induce sweat and relieve pain. This may not have been an original Inuit remedy, as I believe such a treatment was common in parts of Germany; early German missionaries might have introduced it to Labrador.

They were also great believers in the value of rodent skins for healing wounds. The skin of a freshly-killed mouse, placed over a wound with the fur outside, was said to promote healing. Mouse skins were also used as a dressing for glandular swellings, perhaps because they kept the gland warm.

They had an astounding method of removing foreign bodies from the eye. First they obtained a louse, not a difficult assignment in earlier times, and tied a woman's hair around it. When this delicate task was done, they placed the louse directly on the eyeball, letting it drag the hair behind. The hair swept the foreign body from the eye. This incredible procedure, which seems to smack of medieval quackery, was said to be almost infallible. I have not seen it myself, though Reverend Hettasch and Pa Perrett both had. I reported the practice in the journal of the Canadian Medical Association, where it was not challenged though it provoked some surprise.

Strangely, the Inuit seem to have had no remedy for impetigo, which was common among them. We successfully treated this condition with vitamins, soap and water, though it did sometimes prove stubborn.

A cure for headache which persists to this day was to tie a tight band around the forehead. Relief is said to follow within a few hours.

In earlier times, the Inuit shamans were reputed to cure people by the power of suggestion. They were said to be able to kill people by the same means. Predictably, they clashed with missionaries. Countering the shaman's claim to be able to kill by magic was the missionary's declaration that sinners would burn in hell. The shamans fought a losing battle, as the missionaries promised not only bodily cures but release from the fear of vengeful spirits which ruled the lives of pagan Inuit.

By appointing a surgeon and physician, Dr. Christopher Brasen, as the first superintendent of its Mission on the coast of Labrador, the church recognized that healing the body was as important as saving souls and that in its missionary effort science and religion must go hand in hand.

So it was that for more than 180 years, until 1954, Moravian missionaries were largely responsible for the medical needs of Inuit and settlers of northern Labrador. The number of well-thumbed medical books in the Mission's libraries attest to their interest in this work. Only during the last half-century of this period were they assisted by the annual and sometimes biannual visits of personnel from the International Grenfell Association, and by medical students and nurses on the government mail boat.

While they were grateful for the medical efforts of missionaries, Inuit swarmed upon any visitor whose name proclaimed him a doctor, whether of medicine, divinity, philosophy or music. Many a visiting Ph.D. has had trouble explaining why he could not offer the treatment, sometimes even the surgery, expected.

In 1940, when I returned to England to marry Doris, our honeymoon was a six-month course at the Missionary School of Medicine in London. This institution, though inferior to Livingston College, offered crash courses in simple medicine, very minor surgery and first aid for theology students whose work would take them to tropical climates. It was amazing how much they packed into the course, even if much of it was useless in the sub-Arctic.

The school taught homeopathic remedies and theory. Homeopathy is the treatment of illness by minute doses of drugs which, in a healthy person, would produce symptoms like those of the illness at hand. While I still do not entirely agree with this approach, I must admit that some remedies were amazingly effective. Homeopathy has the added virtue that all its remedies are foolproof, which cannot be said of conventional medicine.

As the years passed and we came to know our patients better, my wife and I had fair success with our medical work. Gradually our knowledge grew and our techniques improved. Doris in particular became a very good diagnostician. With the coming of mercy flights and, later still, air ambulance service, our patients had a fighting chance of surviving even such critical ailments as acute appendicitis. One of my colleagues, the Reverend George Harp, once amputated an arm with the aid of the local Hudson's Bay manager, Hayward Haynes. Paul Hettasch, under the supervision of Dr. Wilfred Grenfell, removed an eye. Doris and I undertook nothing so radical but we treated bullet wounds and performed minor surgery. Our one major advantage over visiting doctors was that we knew our patients intimately. We were often able to advise doctors and nurses not only on the medical history of patients but on their intolerance of certain medicines. Several times doctors on coastal boats or scientific expeditions sought our advice on treatment of their own crews.

My growing fluency in Inuktut was of great assistance in this medical work. However, in 1941 a group of almost starving Indians from Sept-Iles, Quebec, appeared in Nain. While they had taken some fur, their long trek through the barren interior had been mostly unproductive. The storekeeper, who professed some knowledge of their language, brought the chief and several members of his band to the mission house so that Doris and I might attend to their medical needs. Our interpreter soon discovered that the language of trade has little use in the practice of medicine. When his desperate efforts got us nowhere, I tried Inuktut, but with no more success.

Finally we resorted to sign language, man's oldest form of communication, and were amazed at our success. When we had supplied them with the medicines they needed we sat back, feeling quite satisfied, to share a pot of tea. At the end of their visit the chief, whose unlikely name was Austin and who had sat through our antics without expression, lifted his disreputable hat with some flourish and said, in good English, smiling only slightly, "Thank you, sir. Thank you, madam. We are most grateful to you both."

I have never been sure whether he was too polite to admit his knowledge of English after we were launched into our charades and sign language, or whether he enjoyed watching us make fools of ourselves.

Missionaries, shamans, visiting doctors and Ph.Ds were not the only ones to practise medicine among the Inuit. There were also the *akiterijut*, who were equivalent to chiropractors in our culture. Claiming a deep knowledge of anatomy, they diagnosed some ills as being caused by the displacement of organs and bones from their proper positions. Their remedies, restoring these parts to their place by manipulation, were sometimes more brutal than a football scrimmage on third down. There is no doubt that some of their rough treatments were effective, but both missionaries and some Inuit believed they had caused miscarriages. Nevertheless they remained a popular source of treatment until the late 60s and may indeed still flourish, for there are people everywhere who resort to quacks and charlatans.

There were also Inuit who practised dentistry of a sort. I was compelled to resort to one of these myself during my first winter in Hopedale. Tom, the "dentist", manhandled my aching molar until he triumphantly removed what was clearly just part of it. However, this cured the ache and a visiting dentist got the rest of the tooth the following summer.

In Nain, a man named Josua Panniok was my competitor in both dentistry and medicine. He was an elderly widower who lived alone in a little house which was always scrupulously tidy. He never hunted; I do not recall that he even had a gun. He did fish in the summer, sometimes with another man and sometimes alone in his little boat. Apart from that, he seemed to spend nearly all his time fetching the wood he cut and split to heat his house. One year he had a single dog harnessed to his short sled, but mostly he manhauled the sled to and from the forest, several miles from the village. Sometimes children helped him, chatting pleasantly the whole time, ignoring his silence; Josua was almost stone deaf. How long he had been afflicted I do not know, but it seemed to have been a long time because his speech was difficult to follow. I dealt with him as everyone did, by shouting and making signs. I think I was the only person who called him Josua; to everyone else he was Panniok.

He had a reputation for being able to pull teeth painlessly without an anaesthetic; many who objected to my injections went to him. However, he was hampered by his deafness. On one occasion a man came to me furious because Josua had pulled the wrong tooth. When the patient complained, Josua became very angry. He shouted and indeed threw his bloody forceps at the startled victim. This conduct was quite out of character, and offended the patient as much as the loss of a good tooth.

Josua's deafness worried him, but one day he announced in triumph that he had found a remedy. The cure was mother's milk, squirted into the ear from source. Naturally this became the talk of the village and a number of spectators gathered when Josua recruited a young nursing mother for this operation. I was not among them, but several told me what followed.

Panniok sat on a chair and the young woman stood beside him. She bared one of her breasts, bent over, placed the nipple in his ear and squeezed. The result was dramatic. Josua jumped to his feet, knocking over his chair and almost felling his donor. Shouting loudly, he dashed from the house and ran through the village, still yelling, followed by spectators who were sure he had gone mad.

A couple of men caught him, took him by the arms and led him home. He went calmly. Arriving home, he sat for a time on the side of his bed. He put his head in his hands as if in deep thought, perhaps meditating on the failure of his astounding remedy. Then a smile spread across his face as he lifted his head. He began to chuckle, and was soon laughing heartily.

Maybe it was all a joke! We never knew.

When I took over the medical work in my district the older missionaries told me the Inuit did not suffer either cancer or appendicitis. Yet in my first year among them, I had reason to doubt both claims.

In the winter of 1936 I was called to treat an elderly man named Migaile Nochasak. When I examined him it seemed to me, from my reading and limited knowledge, that he was facing a major abdominal catastrophe. With the arrival of the first boat I sent him to Cartwright Hospital, where his disorder was diagnosed as abdominal cancer. As far as I know this was the first confirmed case of cancer among the Labrador Inuit. By that time they had been exposed to the white man's diet for over one hundred years, though they did not eat much store-bought food except when game was scarce.

Several years later I was able to contribute a very small part to a book entitled, "Cancer, a Disease of Civilization", written by the famous explorer Vilhjalmur Stefansson. He had previously written a book called "The Fat of the Land", and the theme of both was that the traditional Inuit diet contributed to a life in which cancer and many other white men's ills played no part. I believe this was true.

There were a few cases of cancer among the settlers. The first confirmed case was that of a man named William Ford, who died in about 1925. Earlier cases may have gone unrecognized. Ford had several wives, the last of whom, a young Inuit woman named Lea, also died in the early 1940s of cancer of the womb. Over the years, there was an increasing incidence of cancer, especially among the women. Although the Inuit are heavy smokers, only in comparatively recent years have they taken up tailor-made cigarettes. Formerly the inconvenience of smoking a pipe or rolling their own cigarettes discouraged chain smoking. With increasing use of tailor-made cigarettes among both sexes, we may expect an increase in the incidence of lung cancer in the years to come.

Appendicitis was almost unknown among the Inuit. However in the death records of the Moravian Mission, which go back over two hundred years, the phrase, "Cause of Death: Abdominal Disorder" keeps recurring. It seems likely that at least a few of these deaths were caused by acute appendicitis.

Undoubtedly some of the others arose from botulism, a virulent form of food poisoning. Its cause was the Inuit love of very high meat, and impatience in its preparation. One such dish is *igunak*, meat which has been buried to induce decay. Another is *udjak*, meat which is not cooked but putrified by the application of low heat. This was popular among the Inuit from the more northerly communities.

In 1956, six out of nine people who ate *udjak* at a hunting camp twenty-five miles from Nain died of botulism. One of those who survived did so because he ate sparingly. When the others collapsed he was able to seek help. This man and two others survived after treatment at the hospital in Nain.

Dr. John Brocklehurst, formerly of the Grenfell Mission, wrote a short history of this case for the British Medical Association Journal using information I supplied. In it, he dismissed the Inuit belief that *udjak* made in wooden containers is safe while the same dish made in metal containers can be fatal. Yet I am convinced there was some truth to this. The issue was not simply wood vs. metal, for it was generally believed that enamel containers were safe unless the enamel was chipped. In any case, there were at least twenty deaths from botulism during my thirty-six years in Labrador.

One of the most enduring tragedies was the high infant mortality among the Inuit. A search of Mission records, which go back to 1771, shows that in some years one infant in every three would die before its first birthday. The number went even higher during the years when measles, flu and other imported diseases swept through the Inuit population.

Although some of the missionaries tried to give prenatal care, this was hampered by the semi-nomadic life of the Inuit and the interference of native midwives and *akiterijut*. However, I was able to conduct fairly successful prenatal classes in the largely settler village of Makkovik in the winter of 1939. I was assisted by Miss Bertha Andersen, the sixty-year-old village midwife.

Confederation of Newfoundland with Canada in 1949 brought

increased medical aid by air. This, together with higher incomes, contributed to a great reduction in infant mortality, at least south of Nain. Improved services in native communities were financed by the Federal Government under the terms of Confederation. Tuberculosis was brought more or less under control in this period. Since 1942, the Royal Canadian Air Force and sometimes the U.S. Air Force had been making occasional mercy flights from the new air base at Goose Bay. However, Confederation saw the organization of an air ambulance service which enabled the Grenfell doctors to make more frequent visits and to hold fairly regular clinics on the coast. This greatly eased the work of the missionaries, and of course contributed to the health of residents.

For many years, however, medical and dental work demanded a great deal of my time, and put me on call twenty-four hours a day. The variety of cases was astonishing, and I propose to devote the next few pages to examples.

Soon after my first trip to Nain I encountered my first major case of frostbite. Two young Hopedale men, Sam Torarak and Manasse Pijogge, had gone off "wooding." They expected to return the same evening, but were caught by a very bad blizzard early that afternoon.

It is easy to be lost this way. The morning might dawn with all the promise of a glorious day, but lowering clouds build swiftly, the snow begins to fall soft and quiet as a benediction and then the wind begins, softly at first but soon with frightening force, until travellers move within a small, howling space occupied only by the sled and themselves, drawn by dogs obliterated from their vision. On such a day were Sam and Manasse lost. They did not return that night, and continuing blizzard made a search impossible for the next two days. The church bells rang constantly throughout the day and far into the darkness in the hope that the boys might be near the village. It was a vain hope, and the clang of the bells was lost in the clamour of the wind.

The third day dawned bright and clear, and a search party soon found the lost young men. They had huddled in sleeping bags in the blinding storm and Sam had shielded his companion with his own body. While Manasse was only slightly frozen, Sam was in desperate shape, quite unable to move his frozen legs. I worked frantically to thaw them out, and to make him as comfortable as possible. In the following days, though he had escaped gangrene, Sam was unable to walk. Day after day I massaged his feet and legs, until finally he was able to stand with the aid of two sticks. Early in June, after

I had put in three months work on Sam's feet and legs, we had a visit from a doctor. He told us that Sam might be able to walk with crutches someday, but only with much difficulty and pain. This renewed the challenge; Sam and I continued the daily massage and exercises. Six weeks later he was walking, though with a limp. Today he still walks flatfooted and awkwardly, but he walks.

Epidemics were a major source of grief. I had heard of the appalling impact of the Spanish flu which hit Labrador late in 1918. As a boy in England I went through this worldwide epidemic myself and knew how devastating it had been in Europe, but what I learned of the epidemic in Labrador was almost beyond belief. The village of Okak, with a population of 263, was left with fifty-six alive.

The flu had apparently reached the coast from the mission ship, the *Harmony*, but its effect was delayed. The people of Okak had scattered to their fall and winter sealing and trapping places before illness struck. When many of those left in the village became ill and died, the missionaries set out to visit people in the outlying camps. They were met with scenes which defy description. The bodies of the dead had been attacked by ravenous dogs which had broken into houses. The few living were so weak and emaciated they looked scarcely alive. In one home a baby girl was alone with the bodies of her entire family. She was rescued and lives today in Nain. The epidemic was the death of Okak, for the survivors moved away, some to Hebron but most to Nain and a few to Hopedale.

During my years in Nain I was called upon several times to deal with epidemics, but none like that one. The worst was in 1942. The Newfoundland Commission of Government had taken over the stores from the Hudson's Bay Company, and spring found them poorly stocked. There were more supplies in Hopedale than in Nain, so our storekeeper arranged to get flour and molasses from Hopedale. Five or six dog teams left to get it. They arrived in Hopedale just when people who had been working at the new air base in Goose Bay returned for a visit. Some of them had flu, which the visitors from Nain unknowingly picked up.

They loaded each *komatik* with several barrels of flour and set out for Nain just before Easter. Several became ill on the trip and were unable to handle their unwieldy loads, so they cached the flour and dashed for Nain as quickly as their dogs could carry them. Eventually all arrived, but several were desperately ill.

At first it seemed the sickness would be confined to the men who had returned from Hopedale and a few members of their immediate families. Then people who had been away at their trapping places for most of the winter began returning for Easter, a time of great celebrations in Nain. There were also visitors from the north. Now there were almost four hundred people in the village, compounding the overcrowding in many homes. Doris wrote:

> In one house there were five families living and it was there that the epidemic first started to spread. Bill did his best to try and stop people from visiting the sick and so carrying the infection, and for a while we were hopeful that it might be isolated, but it suddenly broke out in a number of houses simultaneously and by the end of the week there must have been well over one hundred cases, including the Hettasch family.

Suddenly what had been a few isolated cases of influenza flared into a major epidemic. By the Saturday before Palm Sunday more than two-thirds of the village was sick. I was obliged to cancel the most important religious services of the year.

By Monday there were only sixteen of us on our feet. These were Inspector Rockwood of the Newfoundland Rangers, his wife Senneth, my wife Doris, a teacher named Anne Smith, eleven Inuit and settlers, and myself. Together we organized relief. The women made soup and baked bread, while the men kept fires going in the homes of the stricken. A woman named Miriam Torarak tended the sick. At night, exhausted, I would fall into bed only to be awakened by another call.

> From early morning until late at night Bill was out doing what he could. We ransacked the house for bedclothes and took covers off our own beds for the sick. It was nothing to find a woman and two children sleeping in a single bed. I packed all the feathers I had saved into clean flour bags to make pillows. We made pneumonia jackets out of cotton wool and guaze.

> Our kitchen was a communal soup kitchen and we baked bread every day. In many houses there was nobody to cook or do anything. Bill had to see that each house had water and wood. He had to find boys to empty slop buckets and make splits. He even had to light the fires in some of the houses. All our bottled meat had to be used to make soup. I used to mince the meat up finely and divide it between my two big boilers. Fortunately we still had dried onion and some gravy flavouring and we managed to make soup enough. I had plenty of rice which I had been keeping for the time when we should be out of potatoes. I had ordered a dou-

ble quantity of cereals last fall, so I had plenty . . . . The baby was only three weeks old when we took her. Both her parents had flu and there was no one to care for her as both parents were orphans. Unfortunately Keto and Gilbert (the parents) developed pneumonia. They have no home of their own and apparently gave the flu to the two other occupants of the house . . . Gilbert had been in bed with TB for the greater part of the winter and he did not really stand a chance of recovering, although he lingered for quite a while. In the end he turned round and blamed Bill for keeping him on earth so long.

On Good Friday our patients began dying. We lost five in twenty-four hours, and from then on we fought a losing battle. By the time the epidemic ended a month later twenty-two people had died. Doris described one case in a letter:

> One of our chapel servants died five days after his remarriage. He had lost his wife and baby six weeks before. The waiting period before remarriage after the death of a spouse is six weeks. I think he should have been in bed instead of being married—in fact Bill told him so—but he was terribly anxious to be married before Easter because he had four children.

All those who died were Inuit except the last, a strong, good man named Tom Flowers. He had been my right hand during the last three weeks of the epidemic. A modest, quiet man, Tom had been a sniper in France during World War I. He moved about the village throughout the sickness, appearing wherever he was wanted, doing whatever was needed without fuss or comment, stretching out his hands in merciful comfort.

One of his own daughters, sixteen-year-old Mikkijok, had died earlier in the epidemic. This attractive young woman knew she was dying and begged me to sit with her. Weary and overwhelmed by the immensity of the task I was facing, I could not deny her request and sat with her for several hours, holding her hand as her life slipped away. At the beginning of her illness she had been confident she would recover; now that she was gone my sense of failure was almost more than I could bear. Yet I had to go on fighting for the others.

Tom's death struck me equally hard. This good man had stood by me so many times in the past weeks as together we watched friends "walk through the valley of the shadow of death." Now he walked that valley himself and failed to return.

At the height of the epidemic in April, Inspector Rockwood and I were criticised for banning all travel from Nain to Nutak and Hebron, the villages north of the Kiglapait Mountains. This prevented the delivery of mail, which displeased the whites in the north, but it kept the epidemic out of villages where its effects would have been devastating. Doris wrote:

> The evening Andrease died, Bill and Inspector Rockwood wired out to try and get medical aid and medicines by plane. No reply came during that next terrible week. Five people died in two days and Bill was nearly frantic with lack of sleep, overwork and worry. He decided to wire again and a reply came back that medicines were being sent.

The worst was over before any help arrived from outside. Feeble survivors began to improve on their own with the warmer spring weather. Luckily the sea ice moved out early that year. The first ship, the *Winnifred Lee*, arrived with salt for the fishery and bags of flour for Richard White, a private trader in Kauk, near Nain. Captain Joshua Winsor of the *Winnifred Lee* bought back twenty bags of the flour he had just delivered and gave them to the store manager in Nain for distribution to the people. This was only one of the many kindnesses done for the people of northern Labrador by the Winsor family.

No sooner had the ship gone than a Royal Canadian Air Force plane came in to bring help for those who had not fully recovered, and to bring us a supply of sulfa drugs, at that time a "miracle drug." Doris wrote:

> It was just a fortnight after the original message was sent that the plane came. We were terribly relieved when she landed, bringing a doctor with her. I opened my last bottle of partridges, cooked my last potatoes and opened my last tin of peas for dinner. The doctor was young and very "interested" in the epidemic, but when he came the worst was over and in most cases he told us to continue our treatment.

But the enemy was not yet exhausted. The flu struck back at the end of August, when most of the people of Nain were out at their fishing places. Inspector Rockwood and I steamed from camp to camp, helping the sick, and for awhile the epidemic seemed to subside. When it broke out again with renewed fury, Doris and I travelled out to bring the sick back to the village. Death stalked again, and a further nineteen people died.

With the coming of fall, the illness subsided once more and people began to recover their strength. Life became easier.

In later years we had other epidemics of flu, measles and diphtheria, but by then help was more readily available from the Canadian and U.S. air forces and later from the air ambulance service of the International Grenfell Association. After 1942 the mercy flights of the air forces became a regular feature of our life. The Inuit and settlers owe much to the airmen of Goose Bay. In one year Lieutenant Freddy Tuplin of the RCAF made eighteen mercy flights to Nain alone. I am proud to report that in every case the senior medical officer at the base confirmed our diagnosis. Apart from Freddy Tuplin, I remember with deep gratitude Group Captain Burchal, Squadron Leader Ted Snider, Lieutenant Al Cheeseman and others who served us in those times.

Although Doris and I quickly gained experience in treating common disorders, we continually faced new situations. These demanded not only common sense but constant reference to our growing collection of medical books and our invaluable Merck Manual.

Burns, frostbite and gunshot wounds were some of the forms which tragedy took. One year the last boat brought the usual supply of tobacco for those who rolled their own cigarettes, but this year for the first time the packets of loose tobacco failed to contain a pack of cigarette papers. There were some in the store, but by Christmas these were gone. One young man from our congregation decided to travel north to Nutak, a distance of almost one hundred miles, to buy cigarette papers. It was an ill-conceived idea, but he was not to be dissuaded. He took his seventeen-year-old brother along.

It had been easy going on the journey north, and they had bought a large supply of papers and started home. All went well for the first two days of their return, until they started down Manowa Brook, on the southern slopes of the Kiglapaits. Here, unknown to them, there were several places in the brook where the ice was "hung up." The ice had formed when the water was higher, but when it subsided the ice remained as a brittle crust with nothing beneath it. Steering their *komatik* along the rough and twisting watercourse, they broke through such a place and were plunged into water above their waists.

Scrambling out, they knew they had to pitch camp to get dry. They gathered wood for a fire but discovered with a shock that their only matches were wet and useless. By the time they pitched their tent and changed into spare clothing, the frost was taking hold of their lower limbs. Too tired to move on, they slept fitfully.

When they woke, they knew their only hope was to make it to the nearest house, about twelve miles away in Webb's Bay. The older brother's feet were frozen and the younger was quite incapable of walking. Clumsily and painfully the older man lashed his brother to the *komatik*. After steering the sled down the frozen brook to the sea ice, the driver harnessed himself and stumped along with the dogs, knowing his brother desperately needed help.

After a tortuous journey they reached the Webb home. Seeing the driver's distress, the Webbs helped him into the house, where he told them his brother was lashed in blankets on the *komatik*. The young man was already dead. As the Webbs thawed the older brother's feet the pain became unbearable and he begged for a knife to cut them off. When he had rested awhile they brought him to Nain.

By the time I saw him, gangrene had already set in. I was able to get a mercy flight from Goose Bay, and within a few hours he was in the RCAF hospital there. He was later transferred to the International Grenfell Association hospital in St. Anthony, where one leg was amputated just below the knee, the other half way up the thigh. The Ladies' Auxiliary of the RCAF in Goose Bay raised the funds for his first pair of artificial limbs.

Death and trouble seem to stalk some families, but especially the unwary. Not long after this incident, the mother and sister of these two young men were living at a camp some distance from Nain. The daughter went out hunting shore birds with a .22 and returned to the house with the rifle still cocked and loaded. It went off as she tried to uncock it, and shot her mother in the abdomen. The mother died in their boat on the way to Nain.

Knowing that my parishioners deserved more competent medical attention, I never really enjoyed this side of my work. Still less did I like dentistry, but like most missionaries in northern Labrador I frequently filled and extracted teeth, for there was no one else to do such work for about 363 days a year. I had learned the basics in three months with the Reverend Fred Grubb, after the death of his wife in the winter of 1938. He in turn had learned from a Harvard dentist visiting Labrador one summer.

One day when I had been recently instructed on filling teeth, an Inuit lady came into Hopedale from a camp about twenty-five miles distant. Her teeth needed attention. Reverend Grubb looked into her mouth, drew back somewhat hurriedly and referred her to me. I soon learned the reason. This lady (I'll call her Mary) had a formidable case of bad breath. However, I gritted my teeth and filled hers. She was pleased with the job, and I was glad to have passed another milestone in my medical training.

Two weeks later I was visiting families in the outlying camps and came to the home of this patient. My driver and I were treated to tea, bread, margarine and a big dish of what I took to be some kind of jam. I helped myself liberally, but realized with the first mouthful that this was no ordinary spread. I found it quite distasteful, in fact, but finished it out of courtesy to my host. When we left the house, I asked my driver what I had been eating. "*Suvalik*," he said, casually. This was troubling news.

"Who made it, do you think?"

"Oh," he said, "I expect it was Mary." On hearing this my stomach rebelled, for I knew something of the preparation of this dish. It is made of fish roe, red berries, fermented seal oil and prechewed blubber. I would sooner not have known that Mary chewed the blubber.

On another occasion, visiting Voisey's Bay from Nain, a sturdy Indian came to me for an extraction. I had forceps but no pain-killer, having used the last at my previous stop. I explained this to my patient, but he insisted he would need no anaesthetic. In the face of such courage I could scarcely refuse, though both his size and that of the ailing tooth alarmed me. I had never seen such a molar.

Reluctantly I set about the task. I used every trick I knew, and all my strength, but that tooth would not budge. I was panting but my patient never turned a hair. At last I straightened up, admitting defeat. The Indian was made of sterner stuff and insisted I continue. Frankly I was scared: scared to refuse and scared to continue, scared of the damage I might do his mouth and the damage he might do me.

I renewed my struggle after a bit of a rest and finally held aloft that huge, stubborn tooth. As I examined his bleeding jaw with bruised fingers, the Indian complimented me on my skill. He was lying, of course, but I welcomed the courtesy.

Sometimes I was called to treat Newfoundlanders fishing in the area from their schooners. One glorious summer morning the skipper of the *Winifred Lee* called the store in Nain from Hopedale with the request that I go to Queen's Lakes to treat a schoonerman with an injured arm. I set out with an Inuit boatman to make the thirty-mile journey in an open trap boat. Arriving at the schooner I found the man's whole arm swollen to half again its normal size. He had been thrown against a cask of gasoline and had broken the skin, but ignored the injury until it became seriously infected.

I gave the man a massive dose of penicillin and called the RCAF at Goose Bay asking for a mercy flight. It was too late to fly that night, but they assured me the plane would reach the schooner next morning. I returned to Nain and was relieved next morning to see the plane fly over the village on its return to Goose Bay. I turned on my radio receiver and picked up the pilot calling my station. He said he had a doctor with him who wished to assure me that the patient was aboard and that my treatment had probably saved the man's arm, if not his life.

Our medical work, which covered nineteen of my thirty-six years in Labrador, was a blend of success, frustration and failure. Success was sweet, but our failures left me feeling drained and impotent. Nevertheless I am certain there are people who would not be alive today were it not for our efforts, especially Doris's skill in diagnosis. Looking back, I realize that we learned much from visiting doctors, especially our dear friend, Dr. Tony Paddon, who always found time to help and who often referred to me as his favourite witch doctor. We were lucky, too, to be able to consult Paul Hettasch, who shared the results of his vast experience with us. Yet even when we became fairly competent in our medical work, it was a burden. In 1953 we gratefully turned it over to a qualified and very capable nurse.

11

OF LIGHTER THINGS

Although our work as missionaries kept us busy, there were times of leisure and pursuits unconnected with the church or the community. My older colleagues believed one needed a hobby to survive in the north, and with most of them it was gardening. While I enjoyed my wife's pleasure in this pursuit, I could not fully share their enthusiasm and looked elsewhere for diversion.

When I first arrived in Hopedale in 1935, Pa Perrett took me to visit his "beetle traps," large stones which he visited regularly to collect the bugs sheltering beneath them. He also collected moths, butterflies and birds' eggs, probably on behalf of some university or museum. In addition, he collected stamps, confining himself chiefly to those which were unusual and rare. This was an enthusiasm he shared with the late Canon Rusted of Carbonear.

Paul Hettasch was interested in the flora and birds of the north, and had a wide knowledge of the edible fungi. He also collected moths and butterflies.

It was notable that few of the missionaries in my time showed any enthusiasm for hunting and fishing. It was not until I married that I took much interest in the outdoors, and I was never enthused by hunting or fishing. Hunting, especially, was repugnant to me for I hated taking life of any sort, or almost any. I confess that I had no mercy for mosquitoes and blackflies.

I do remember one hunt, though, which occurred soon after I brought Doris to Nain. We were invited to join some friends in hunting ducks from a boat. Doris had never handled a gun and I was a poor teacher. I was constantly turning aside her .22, which she carried quite stylishly but which I often found pointed at my stomach. There were no ducks, though they would have been perfectly safe. Eventually someone shot a loon and we felt compelled to cook it. Even after several hours of cooking it was so tough as to be almost inedible, and revenged itself by giving us indigestion. What little liking I had for the chase was cured by this incident and in the next thirty years I did not shoot even a half dozen birds.

In fact, I had no real hobby in the sense of a serious pursuit outside of work. My chief interests were the Inuit language and the people themselves. For some years, however, the running of my little radio station became an absorbing offshoot of my work. The origins of this station make a curious story.

In 1948 I received a letter from an American electronics expert named M.W. Ogletree who had worked in Labrador with the U.S. Coast Guard during World War II, installing Loran stations on the coast. He knew that a small radio station in Nain would be of inestimable value to the work of the Mission. He was willing to buy the equipment and set it up if we could find about two thousand dollars. He himself was willing to work for the Mission for a small wage, and his wife Connie would accept a teaching position in the Nain school.

By the same mail I received a letter from the Mission Board telling me that a Scottish nobleman, Lord McRay, had offered our Mission two thousand dollars if we could find an appropriate use for this sum. Could we ever!

The affair was settled by mail, funds were transferred to the U.S., and Ogletree purchased a transmitter, receiver and small push button receivers from military surplus. We agreed to hire Ogletree as my special assistant and Connie as a teacher for the 1949-50 school year. Returning from a short visit to England, Doris and I arrived back in St. John's in the summer of 1949 in time to meet them there, to expedite the equipment through customs and to lobby for a radio licence. This was granted largely, I believe, thanks to the support of Joseph R. Smallwood, who had just recently led the province into Confederation and become its first premier.

Early in 1950 our radio station began limited operation, contacting the RCAF in Goose Bay with requests for medical aid. Ogletree adapted the small push-button radios for use in our area, and we distributed them to Inuit families living at places distant from Nain.

By the time the Ogletrees completed their contracts in July, 1950, everything was set up for regular broadcasts. During the summer while the Inuit were away fishing, we broadcast two church services every week. By the end of August I had planned a schedule of broadcasts for the next nine months, and on the first of September we began nightly broadcasts of news, entertainment and educational programming. Programmes were in Inuktut and English. This added an additional heavy load to my work, but I had tremendous help from the Mounties Blake MacIntosh and Joe Butt, as well as from the Inuit and other whites in the settlement. Joe Butt became responsible for station maintenance, a function taken over by other Mounties when he and Blake left. Martin Martin and Gerry Sillitt were two of the Inuit who helped with the station, while storekeeper Max Budgell and his wife Lucy, and the bilingual teacher Beatrice Ford, also helped a great deal.

We broadcast music, plays, vocalists, religious programmes, talks and of course the news. Roughly seventy-five per cent of our content was in Inuktut.

Translating news was not easy, for much of it dealt with a world remote from the experience as well as the vocabulary of our listeners. I had real trouble with the word "communist." Finally I Eskimoized the word to "*Kommunistit,*" gave a long talk on its evils and knew that if nothing else our listeners would soon know that the "*Kommunistit*" were the bad guys and the "*Demokrasisit*" the good guys. One day I overheard a man calling his neighbour a *Kommunistialuk*, a horrible communist. In time the word became an expletive right along the northern Labrador coast!

Over the years we broadcast the performances of an Inuit choir; historical plays with an Inuit cast; biographies and simple scientific talks; evening devotions, sometimes conducted by Inuit; and an Inuit-white group singing western music. We were in daily radio contact with the RCAF in Goose Bay, supplying reports of ice and weather conditions.

This continued for more than seven years, during which we never knew if we were operating within the terms of our licence. We did know, however, that this was a unique and valuable service to the Inuit from Hebron to Goose Bay. We we did it all with volunteers, at no cost either to the audience or to ourselves except for the cost of fuel to charge the station batteries.

In a similar vein, from 1955 to 1957 Max Budgell and I produced a monthly newspaper called the *Nainemiok*, distributed free of charge.

This provided Inuit and whites with a platform from which to air their views on local affairs, a contribution to democratic local government.

After Doris joined me in Nain, I began to share her interest in botany and wildflife. Even in winter, when the landscape is almost uniformly white and bare, we found things of interest. For example, walking on snowshoes through the woods we discovered a complex network of passages beneath the surface of the snow, where mice went about their business hidden from the eyes of predators.

The winter also gave wonderful displays of Northern Lights. The Merry Dancers, as they have been called by some Indian groups, did indeed dance across the skies and produce an amazing variety of colours, from dark red to light green. Some have claimed that the lights make a sort of crackling sound, but I never heard it. However, since they were usually at their best on cold, crisp nights, it could be that the frosty atmosphere produced the sounds attributed to the lights. There was a belief among some of the northern folk that it was dangerous to whistle while the aurora display was at its height, as one might "whistle down" the lights and suffer bodily harm. Though not a good whistler, I believe I have disproved this superstition.

The changing face of the northern landscape was always a source of wonder and excitement. After a blizzard, the wind-sculpted snow displayed forms of indescribable beauty. The snow was never dead white but blended shades of pale greens and blues. Toward evening, gorgeous pinks appeared. Because I do not really appreciate things when I am alone, all the charms of the northern landscape took on new meaning for me now that I had a loved one with whom I could share it and through whom I could see new forms of beauty.

During the summer we often wandered through the woodland looking for birds. One day we were disappointed by the absence of birds normally common there, until we saw the cause; a great northern shrike, or butcher bird, had taken possession of our little grove. The shrike catches small birds and impales them on thorns or spiked branches, then devours them. The presence of this marauder annoyed us both. Following him through the woods we discovered his nest in a slender larch. I decided to dispose of the nest. The tree was too slender to climb, yet the nest was too high to reach. I shook the tree as vigorously as I could, hoping to dislodge the nest. I had not reckoned with the shrike, which flew screaming from the nest and dove at me. I hastily withdrew and returned for another try, with the same result, and again for a third before I gave up, leaving the butcher bird to its murderous career.

Occasionally we spotted rare visitors to our land. On one occasion, Doris was following the sound of a ruby-crowned kinglet while I dawdled behind. Suddenly I saw a flash almost like flame, a startling sight amid the sombre shades of black spruce. Then I saw it light on a tree, an astonishing flame-coloured bird. I dashed off to get Doris, who was equally excited. Later we identified it as a summer tanager. How this southern bird made its way to the woods at Nain was a mystery, but we saw it more than once. We could well understand why Indians called this the fire bird.

Other rare visitors we identified include Greenland wheatears, a mourning dove, the occasional bald eagle and even, on one unforgettable day, a pair of beautiful and graceful gyrfalcons high in the air above us. In Happy Valley our garden drew purple finches and cedar waxwings, which played havoc with our red currant crop, and night hawks. For many years Doris kept a record of the birds we saw. Below is a sample for the spring and early summer of 1954.

Jays and woodpeckers all winter in the woods.

April 7	Large flocks of snowbirds fed around the house.
13	Squawl hawk heard at Northern Point. First gulls seen at Kangeklukuluk (Nain district).
May 2	A few longspurs seen on Nain Hill.
3	May First robin heard.
10	May Fox sparrow heard. Two robins seen Two black-backed gulls. Nain Many squawl hawks. Junco

11	Saw 18 black-backed gulls, four Canada geese and herring gulls.	Salt Water Pond
14	Myrtle warblers heard. More fox sparrows. Many Lapland longspurs.	
17	Wilson's snipe Blue winged teal. Canada goose. Black ducks. Harlequin duck.	Reported from Webb's Bay, near Nain.
18	White crowned sparrows. More snowbirds. Greenland wheatears Northern shrike . . . in woods at Nain.	. . . in Nain village.
20	Myrtle warblers seen. Rusty blackbirds. Fox sparrows seen. Semi-palmated plovers Arctic owl.	. . . Northern Point.
21	Two Canada geese.	
26	Ruby crowned kinglet heard.	
27	Black and white warbler seen. American pipit seen.	
28	Great yellowlegs Large numbers of white crowned sparrows.	. . . Northern Point.
30	Kinglets seen.	
June 4	Robin's nest with eggs	. . . Northern Point.

10	Three rusty blackbirds	
11	June Spruce grouse (male)	. . . Nain woods.
	Summer tanager	. . . Nain woods aftei strong S.W. wind.
12	Two brasswing divers.	
13	Black poll warbler. Spruce grouse (female).	
July 18	Saw 51 red-throated loons between Nain and Hebron. One pair Bruniche's murres near Cape Mugford	

Occasionally we saw black bears, but never close. They appeared to be rather cumbersome, but it was amazing how swiftly they could lope off if one approached them. There were many stories about them, some of them suggesting almost human behaviour. Indeed some of the settlers would not eat black bear because the body, when skinned, was so human. Amos Voisey told of seeing a black bear haul his trout nets, peering around first with his paws shading his eyes as if to make sure the coast was clear. Richard White once had a captive bear cub which was almost like one of the family. Finally, after it had broken into his small warehouse once too often, he asked Adolf Ikkaiatsiak, who worked for him, to take the bear off into the country and leave it there to fend for itself. Adolf did this and hurried home. Next morning the bear was back banging on the warehouse door. White later presented the bear to Sir Wilfred Grenfell, who in turn gave it to Clifton Zoological Gardens in Bristol, England.

During our years in Labrador neither of us ever saw a live polar bear. On one sled trip with Fred Winters of Karmarsuk, we followed polar bear tracks for several hours, but without catching up. We ate the meat of this creature several times, but did not enjoy it. Polar bears had become scarce on the Labrador coast before our time, but a few were killed during the years of our residence in Nain. Jerry Sillitt of Nain had killed his first polar bear when he was thirteen. As was the custom with the first kill, he cut the skin of this huge beast in pieces and gave it out to other hunters, presumably for good luck.

One fall evening a widower from Okak, Dan Korah, returned home from a boat trip to find a polar bear lying on his bed. Leaving the door ajar, he quietly retraced his steps to the boat and loaded his rifle. As he crept back to the house, he heard a noise inside, then a loud crashing as he ran closer. When he reached the house he found that the bear had escaped through a window and had taken part of the frame with it. Dan followed the bear as far as he could before he lost the trail. Back at the house he ruefully surveyed the damage, then burst out laughing; there was a large wet spot in the bed. Whenever he retold the story later, Dan said he didn't mind giving comfort to a weary bear, but he thought it unreasonable that his guest should beat up the house and pee in the bed.

Somewhere near Dan's house, I believe on Okak Island, there is a large lake said to contain a water monster, which some people claim to have seen. Others deny even hearing about it. The only description I have had of this beast is that it has a large head and a body like a seal.

Black and white spruce are the commonest trees in the sheltered valleys of the Nain area. These two conifers are joined by occasional stands of balsam fir in the more southerly mission stations. Hunters have found small groves of balsam poplar farther inland, along the banks of streams. Very small stands of birch can be found on the sunny slopes of the deepers bays, but they are very rare north of Nain. The commonest birch is the shrubbery, round-leaved dwarf birch (*Betula glandulosa*) which brightens the hillsides in the fall with its gold and crimson foliage.

On rocky hilltops, northern slopes and on the outside islands a number of dwarf Arctic plants flower briefly in late June or early July. There are little snow gentians (*Gentiana nivalis*), single-flowered campanulas (*Campanula uniflora*), sweet-scented rhododendrons (*Rhododendron lapponicum*), pale bog rosemary (*Andromeda glaucophylla*) and the pink flowers of the Arctic rubus.

Fairy white bells of *Cassiope hynoides* cover the moss like foliage growing between the rock layers overhanging the brook. In dim moist spots grows a delicate fern, (*Cystopteus fragilis*) and occasionally yellow-centred

Rhododendron lapponicum

primulas (*Primula farinosa*), with their pale, mealy rosettes of leaves.

At September Harbour, on the islands outside of Nain, grow tufts of creamy Dryas (*Drya integrifolia*), bright blue alpine speedwell (*Veronica alpina*) and golden Arnica (*Arnica alpina*). The snow saxifrage (*Saxifrage nivalis*) grows only about four inches high, scarcely a quarter the height of the same plant in Greenland. Perhaps the greater length of days in the Arctic summer farther north accounts for the difference.

On exposed wet gravel, tufts of purple saxifrage (*Saxifrage oppositifolia*) make a brave show. In drier spots we find delicate clusters of mountain sandwort (*Aranaria groenlandica*), waxy flowered diapensias (*Diapensia lapponica*), cushions of deep rooted moss campion (*Silene acaulis*) and, on the lower sandy patches, alpine azalea (*Loiseleuria procumbus*) with its pink starry blossoms, and a variety of creeping willows of great age.

Diapensia lapponica

There was always some new plant to examine and classify, and we never did master the many varieties of sedges, willows and lichens. We learned to watch for the flowering of the blueberries, blackberries and red berries, and to hope that late frosts would not ruin the delicate bakeapple crop.

We supplemented our diet by collecting quantities of the many varieties of edible mushroom which abound in the woods around Nain. Often we would take an hour or two off, equipped with a one hundred pound flour sack each, and return with both sacks half full of edible mushrooms. Some of these we dried for winter use, while others garnished fish and meat dishes shared with our many summer visitors.

The Inuit enjoyed eating the shoots of certain willow trees with molasses but they would never eat mushrooms, which they called *Satanasib iksivautangit*, seats of Satan. We found that they ate seaweed, too, but only about an inch of the stem of the fifteen to twenty foot *Alaria*, discarding the rest.

Strangely, in all our travels we never saw caribou except from the air. On one occasion, travelling by dogs with Martin Martin, we came upon the tracks of a company of about fifty caribou and followed them to a place where they had recently rested. Martin decided we could not pass this up so we chased after them, following their tracks among the Kiglapait Mountains. We climbed to the tops of mountains; we rushed down the sides of mountains; we travelled along the ridges of mountains, all to no avail. We never even glimpsed a caribou. Martin kept assuring me they were not far ahead but I was not sure. I suspected he enjoyed the chase more than I, and it was obvious that he was much more fit.

I have said earlier that I never enjoyed hunting, though at times I couldn't avoid it. In my first year in Labrador, travelling between Makkovik and Hopedale with two other teams, we were obliged to travel along the edge of the ice, the *sina*, where seals were plentiful. My companions shot more than twenty, but I felt no excitement. In fact I felt rather sick.

Later, while stationed in Nain and travelling on the ice with Lorenz Kojak we sighted a "crawler." This is a seal which has crawled out to bask on the ice, strayed from its breathing hole and cannot find open water. It can only crawl pathetically around in search of the sea. Such seals sometimes get so lost they make their way into woodlands. Their eyes are not adapted to the surface and they apparently mistake the dark band of forest for the blue of open water in the distance. For Lorenz, who needed seal meat, the crawler was a gift. Scenting it, the dogs set off at a furious pace, almost throwing me off the *komatik*. When we drew near, Lorenz threw the *spansel* over the nose of the *komatik* to slow his dogs. Yelling to me to hold them back, he seized the axe and set out after the seal, which made frantic, clumsy but amazingly speedy efforts to escape. But Lorenz overtook it and dispatched it with one blow. There was a great deal of blood and I felt quite sick.

During the winter we had church services four evenings a week and twice on Sundays. Preparation for these alone kept me busy, quite apart from the medical work. Tuesdays there was religious instruction and a service of exposition, which involved discussion and explanation of parts of the Bible. One year I decided to translate parts of Foxe's book of martyrs into Inuktut for use on Tuesdays. Doris was horrified, but my congregation revelled in details of the horrors inflicted upon the Christian martyrs.

We were constantly learning, for we had come to learn as much as to teach. We learned about the country, its friendliness and its cruelty to the ignorant and unwary, its manifold beauties and its awesome storms. We learned about poverty and struggle and above all we learned to love the people among whom we were working.

Excerpts from a letter Doris wrote in September, 1943, in the interval between the epidemics in the spring and fall of that year, describe her first impressions of life in the summer fishing camps in the islands off Nain.

For several weeks Bill has been planning a weekend trip to some of the fishing places but bad weather or lack of fuel prevented it. Last weekend we borrowed the Depot boat on a Saturday afternoon and set off. It was a grand day with a strong, fair wind. We hoisted the sail and we seemed to fly with the waves. We went through narrow, shallow runs between the islands, along coasts of unscalable cliffs to the isolated spots where the people live in tents all the summer fishing for cod.

It was my first experience of this kind and it was quite an education . . . Seven tents constituted quite a village at our first calling place — a bare, exposed spot on the shore of one of the islands. The water was too shallow for the boat to go right in, so punts had to come out . . . . All the paraphernalia of the fishery lined the shore. Drying racks, resembling clothes lines, have long lines of "pipses" (drying cod). Cod's heads were strung together to dry — salting boxes like so many dog kennels — splitting tables — old barrels and a dozen other objects, all strangely pervaded with the odour of fish, proclaimed the occupation of the people. Lazy Eskimo dogs wandered around the tents in search of scraps and offal while the children ran around barefoot over the rocks, very much excited by our arrival.

At our second calling place we put an old blind man ashore with his wife and daughter. He was returning from Nain where he had bid goodbye to his grandson, who is going out to prison. I could not help feeling terribly sorry for the poor old man. It seems that all the summer he sits in his boat and jigs for fish even though he is blind. The other members of his family salt it for him. His sons are not very admirable and this is the second of his grandchildren to be sent to prison.

After leaving this place we were more exposed to the wind and I found the rocking and rolling of the boat a little too much for my tummy so I lay down for a while and I must have fallen asleep. When I awoke it was much colder. Even the character of the islands seemed to have changed and the rocks were worn quite smooth with the grinding of the ice. The lower islands looked like great whale backs shining with the waves washing them. Icebergs shone white in the distance and we passed quite close to a small growler. Our destination was a calm harbour, well-protected between several islands. Three families were fishing here but they were living in wooden houses. In addition one of the Newfoundland fishing schooners was also anchored. Bill said we had passed another in full sail while I was asleep. It is time for them to be going south now.

Martin and his family came out to greet us and escort us to the house. We had a cup of tea and some bread and butter and then we went for a little walk. We climbed the hill behind the house and found that the land was much the same as here in Nain. There were no trees and the shrubs, or rather herbs, grew closer to the ground. Bakeapples were plentiful and we ate all we could find. Some of the plants which are rare in Nain were quite plentiful out there and I think I discovered one new one—a Ranunculus—but I have not been able to make sure yet.

It was a grand evening. The wind had gone down considerably but was just strong enough to keep the flies off us. I had not eaten much when we arrived because I thought we would be having supper as soon as the men finished work. But after we got back there was no sign of a meal, although the seal meat which had been cooking on the stove had disappeared. I was afraid to go and get some food from the boat for fear that Benigna might think me unsociable and unwilling to eat their food, so I was forced to wait with a rolling tummy . . . .

I think at first they were too shy to put seal meat before me but presently we were invited to a meal. After filling my tummy with seal meat, hot, strong tea and bread I felt much more comfortable but exceedingly sleepy, and I was hoping we would be able to get to bed early. The men went on talking and I did my best to carry on a practically monosyllabic conversation with the women. The house only consisted of a large room partially partitioned down the centre and we were to sleep on the floor in the same section as Martin, his wife and daughter and their adopted child, so we could not make a move until they were ready.

I was already finding it difficult to stifle my yawns when the schooner men came ashore. We listened to their family histories, their personal experiences, the experiences of their sons overseas, the history of the Labrador fishery for the last forty years, the change in living conditions in Newfoundland and the increased cost of living; then we were catechised concerning war conditions in England and many other subjects. I had nothing against which I could rest my back. The mosquito bites were irritating madly inside the legs of my boots and my eyelids insisted on drooping. Three or four times the schooner men decided to depart and eventually, when I had almost given up hope, they departed and we had prayers and prepared for the night. We pushed the table and benches into a corner and we three women slept side by side on a big bear skin. Miss Fountain, a teacher from Nain, had Bill's big sleeping bag and I used my down one, while Clara used a couple of blankets. Bill was worst off; he had his head on a pile of wood beside the stove and his feet on our bear skin. Neither of us had much sleep and I was very thankful when dawn came and the day was fine. We washed, and combed our hair, but you don't feel very fresh after a night in most of your clothes. Sanitary arrangements were the most primitive imaginable . . .

After a breakfast of bread and butter, porridge and tea, we wandered out for another walk until church time. The boat had gone off to another nearby fishing place to collect several more families, and when we were eventually ready for service there must have been forty-odd people assembled, all Eskimos. One of the men played the organ which had been rescued from the Nain fire in 1924, and we raised the roof.

Bill had almost finished his sermon when the schooner men walked in — a very much smarter crowd of men than they had been the night before. Their fishy trousers, rubber boots and stained jerseys were gone with their week's growth of beard, and they looked like conventional churchgoers in their Sunday best. Caught on the hop, Bill followed the Eskimo service with a short English service.

All the people were very grateful to us for going and I think they appreciated the visit. We left medicines behind for those with colds, etc., and after another cup of tea we set off on our homeward trip. It took us much longer to get back to Nain although the weather was calm, for we called at all the fishing places *en route*, and at the biggest encampment we held another service in a tent.

Thirty people attended but even now I don't know how they got in. It was only possible to stand upright in the middle of the tent and there were no chairs and only one small bench. The children and some of the women crawled on to the beds on the floor and the rest sat on planks of wood resting on boxes, but they must have had very little room for their knees. Just as we were about to begin, a dog fight started outside and one of the women on the back bench caused a great commotion by her efforts to get out and stop the fight. Eventually the service was ended and we breathed fresh air again . . . .

At our next calling place were two tents and in one we found one of our oldest women, who was bedridden. I think this tent was more unsavoury than any of the others we had seen. The chamber pot had not been emptied and the remains of several meals were left on dirty plates. The two beds were positively filthy and the whole atmosphere made me feel sick . . . . We took her a tin of milk and that was our initial mistake because it reminded her of all the things she wanted. We promised we would do what we could for her and then she wanted medicine. I could not help smiling when she insisted that tobacco was the only medicine which did her chest any good. She produced a much-blackened pipe from among the bedclothes, and Bill gave her a handful of tobacco. When she was quiet enough Bill managed to say a prayer and we departed.

We were going to come straight on to Nain but we were not very far from the place of Old Mike, the oldest man in Nain. We had heard that he was not very well so we decided not to pass him by. It was very calm and warm in the sheltered cove where Mike's dirty little tent stood. It was pathetic to see him in his soiled white sillapak and fur cap, outside a tent made partly of canvas and partly of tarred paper and sods. I think we did some good by going because the store manager later promised to give Mike a new tent. Mike greeted us very enthusiastically and we all sat around on the rocks while Bill prayed. Afterwards the old man asked for a hymn and we sang, then he offered a short prayer after which he began singing another hymn in which we joined. The flies were simply devouring me and I was glad when I was able to move around . . . .

Next week Bill plans to go to some of the settler homes if the weather is good . . . .

Bill has just been called out to settle a dispute between a sick man and his unfaithful wife who has run off to another house with all the bedclothes. He has been gone quite awhile now, so I hope she is not knocking him about too.

Our relations with the Indians, though less constant, were very good. A group of thirteen Indian men appeared in Nain in January, 1941, part of a much larger band who had been travelling from Quebec since the previous summer. They had come out of the country to trade their fur with the Hudson's Bay Company. Doris described them in a letter:

They are quite different from the local Nascopie Indians who seem to be far more primitive . . . . The newcomers are good hunters, tall, fine-featured men with big, dark eyes and long lashes and very high cheekbones. They must have looked very picturesque in their oldtime clothing. Now they are all wearing European clothing. A little farther south there are, we understand, two hundred of them, including women and children, and they have walked last summer a distance approaching two thousand miles. We have had several sprains and ills to attend for the Indians, and the others are waiting until Bill goes south next week on his trip so that he can attend the rest of the sick.

I had already supplied some medicines but thought it best to visit the patients, not only to give further treatment but for my own peace of mind. I therefore arranged with one of the Voisey boys, whose home was very near the Indian camp, to take me there. We arrived at the home of Amos and Emma Voisey after dark, so I was obliged to defer my visit to the Indian camp to the following morning. News of my arrival had travelled before me, for early the next morning three shy Indian youths presented themselves at the Voisey home. They had been sent to escort me and to carry my bag. Edward Voisey was assigned to serve as my interpreter.

The three young Indians set off at a good pace across the rocky terrain behind the Voisey home. It was a clear and frosty morning. As we walked up the gentle slope the animated chatter of the three youths rang out in the morning air. Edward and I were silent, labouring to keep up with the lithe, handsome trio ahead of us, who were soon lost to our sight. When we came over the brow of the hill they rose from the rocks and made a pretence of moving on with great weariness. It was obvious that they were teasing me, mocking my own efforts.

When we finally arrived at the camp, situated in a little clearing in the woods, we were greeted by the chief and two others who appeared to be his right hand men. After a round of formal and rather ceremonial handshaking, they conducted us to the main tent. I was amazed at its size, nearly twenty-five feet long and about half as wide. Its floor was thickly covered with spruce boughs and all around were spread brightly-coloured blankets, on which sat about twenty men. Outside the circle of men sat the women, some of whom were quite lovely. They had set my bag at the middle of the north side of the tent, and the chief motioned me to sit on the blanket beside it.

There was complete silence in the tent as I took my place. No one smiled, but they looked at me with a quiet, impressive dignity. The chief seated himself beside me. Still no one spoke. I wondered what etiquette now demanded. I took my pipe and well-filled tobacco pouch from my pocket, stuffed a little tobacco into the pipe and passed the pouch to the chief on my left. He filled his pipe and passed it on. Since my host did not light his pipe I did not either, but my pouch moved on around the circle and came back to me almost empty. It seemed that the demands of protocol had been met, for the chief now carefully lit his pipe and handed me his matches. I lit mine and soon all the others did the same.

No more than a few puffs had risen before the chief began to speak. There was absolute silence from the others. Edward, sitting on my right, whispered that I was being introduced. I was well known to the Davis Inlet and Voisey's Bay Indians but most of this band were strangers to me. When the chief finished speaking, the seated men greeted me with raised hands. Then, for perhaps three or four minutes, we all smoked in silence, watched by the grave and silent women sitting behind us.

Finally my first patient came forward. This time the chief was my interpreter; there was no need for the absurd charades of our last meeting. It seemed that nearly everyone in the tent had some ill, and when they were finished they fetched the children. It was a tiring session, and it exhausted my stock of medicines.

I started to rise to return to the Voisey home, but the chief quietly and firmly pushed me back to my seat. A drum appeared, and one of the older men started drumming. The blankets were taken up and the dance began. Compared with dances I had seen in movies, this was a most dignified affair, a snakelike and graceful dance in which first only the men took part, while the women clapped to the beat of the drum. Later the women and some of the older children joined the weaving circle, which even that huge tent could scarcely contain. Before it was over only the chief, Edward and I were still seated.

This was my first and only Indian dance, and I left feeling honoured. I was sure the dance had been for me, and I was thankful for the quiet gratitude always shown me when I attempted to practise my slight medical skills among these quiet and dignified people.

Makkovik

12

BY DOG TEAM, BOAT, AND BUSH PLANE

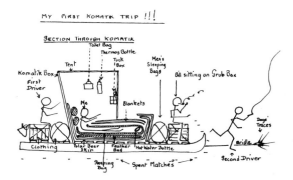

MY FIRST KOMATIK TRIP !!!

After the first trip to Nain and back, my later dog team journeys provided a variety of new experience, exposure to the beauty of northern Labrador, and insights into the skills of my Inuit and settler drivers. Later trips by motor boat, schooner and bush plane gave me greater appreciation of the skill and hardiness of coastal residents, as well as some of the most frustrating and dangerous moments of my life.

It was a common belief that the weather got worse when the missionary travelled, but this bit of folklore took on new force and precision with me. While at first I laughed it off, I came at last to believe it myself, for no rainmaker could claim my success in generating foul weather. Only, it seemed, when Doris travelled with me, as she did sometimes by dog team in spring or by mission plane in winter, could I expect good conditions.

Doris was not entirely pleased with this. She always wanted to spend a night in a snowhouse, the customary shelter for winter travellers caught by a storm, but she never had this experience. With my luck, I did many times.

One trip with Doris in the spring of 1942 took us south to Makkovik, then back through Nain to Hebron, then south again to Nain.

The day we left, immediately after Easter, was idyllic: not a cloud to be seen, not a breath of wind, and perfect ice conditions for travel by sled. It was one of those spring days which brings out all the beauty of the Labrador scene. Doris wrote:

> . . . we set off with 11 dogs, a motley crowd, and two drivers . . . .
> It seemed that half the village jumped on the *komatik* to give us
> a good send off, but they began to drop off one by one. My spirits
> rose up to the skies as the dogs plodded along at a steady pace,
> leaving Nain behind us. We were going to see new faces, different
> scenery, gain fresh ideas and experiences and thoroughly recreate
> ourselves.

We intended to spend the night with our friends Amos and Emma Voisey in Voisey's Bay. As we sped along the ice, a few small pillows of cloud appeared hanging from the arc of heaven. We stopped at Karmarsuk, home of the Winters clan. Edmund Winters, whom I had known in Nain, was dead by this time, but three of his married sons had houses here. From Karmarsuk we proceeded deeper into Voisey's Bay to the home of John Edmunds and his wife, a sister to the Winters boys. We continued on to the home of Emma, a true gentlewoman, and Amos, who both had ancestors from Appledore in Devonshire. They treated us royally, with the best of their food, shelter and entertainment.

The following day we went back down the bay to Keblertaluk, the home of Solomon Edmunds, son of John, and his wife Augusta. Solomon always had the most beautiful huskies in northern Labrador. Proud of his reputation, he was careful to breed his dogs for appearance. Some years he would have a team of pure white animals, and then he would breed for a team of black and whites. For a couple of years I recall he had a team of red dogs. Solomon and Augusta had no children, but they lavished care and attention on their dogs and especially on a mongrel they kept as a house pet. "Troubles" lived up to his name, nipping my heel as I knelt to conduct prayers in the Edmunds home.

From Keblertaluk our progress down the bay was spectacular. The sea ice was like glass, and a following wind caught the *komatik* box cover like a sail, sometimes driving us ahead of the running huskies. The Noa family was not at home at Annaksakarusek, so we continued to Boat Harbour and the warmth of our dear friends, Chesley and Mary Ford.

Still the good weather continued, and we enjoyed another sparkling spring day on our journey to Davis Inlet. There we were greeted by Ralph and Monnie Butt of the Hudson's Bay Company. After the evening meal, Monnie played a musical saw, which I found rather piercing and would avoid if I could do so politely. The Butts had two Indian dogs named "Spring" and "Fall." Because they were leaving Labrador that summer they wanted homes for both. Reluctantly we promised to take "Spring," a dog whose appearance was greatly altered by the Indian belief that lopping off most of a dog's tail and half the ears would prevent distemper. When the Butts left a few months later, they sent us not only Spring but Fall too, and for several years we were blessed and cursed by the presence of two black Indian dogs in our home. Never was there a greater contrast between two animals; Spring was intelligent, quiet, friendly, rather homely and a choosy eater. Fall was handsome but dumb, rambunctious, snappish and voracious.

From Davis Inlet we continued in good weather to Big Bay. As we drew near the portage, Ama Panniguniak, our driver, pointed out a snowy owl standing on top of a branchless, dead tree. Only when we came very close did it stretch its great wings and lazily fly off into the deeper woods, an exquisitely beautiful sight. As Doris wrote:

> My word, what a wingspan it had! I kept my eyes wide open after that. There were white and coloured fox tracks everywhere and on the big lake we saw a red fox which waited until we were almost up to it before it bolted for the woods. Two partridges, a white owl and a coloured fox, and only a quarter of the journey over!

The winding path across the portage and through the heavily wooded country presented little trouble, except for a somewhat barren spot covered with stumps. Coming to a clear place again, our dogs got frisky, running with a liveliness they had not shown since we left Boat Harbour. Galloping ahead of Ama and I, they plunged over what seemed a small cliff, with the *komatik* hurtling behind them. When we caught up, the dogs were spreadeagled in the snow while the *komatik* stood vertically among them, half-buried. Doris perched in the *komatik* box, gazing over this scene as if from a tower.

Everyone was fine, so the incident merely added to the jokes and stories told and retold that night, amid the fiddle music and the songs of another evening with the Broomfields of Big Bay. Doris described that evening in a letter home:

After a meal of seal meat, very well cooked, we talked for a while and then came into the parlour — a big high room . . . with five windows on two sides. An oil lamp was burning on the crimson painted table in the centre of a yellow tablecloth. A crimson floor and skirting board, a roaring iron stove, pink furniture, green and yellow walls, a harmonium, auto harp, violin and accordion, skin rugs and a vivid purple mat all thrust themselves forward. The collection of musical instruments offered an opening and presently we were all sitting around singing cowboy songs to the accompaniment of the autoharp. Talk about a picture of the wild and wooly west! The men were wearing old patched blue overalls and faded, darned jerseys. The girls and their mother sang and tapped their toes to the rhythm. Carrie, the mother, is a tall, well-built woman of Norwegian extraction and two of the girls take after her. All the men are ginger with blue eyes. One could write a book about such a family.

The following day we reached Hopedale, where I met the elders, looked over the Mission accounts and then joined Doris in visiting old friends in the village.

So far our journey had been good, but here there was a change in our fortunes. Our driver, Ama, and his helper Danny were both feeling unwell and Ama was not sure of the route to Makkovik. We therefore decided to hire a team from Hopedale. Our new driver was Bob Winters, who chose as his companion Ben Pardy. Both were of mixed English and Inuit ancestry, unlike Ama and Danny who were pure Inuit. Our new drivers also spoke more English, though they were competent in Inuktut as well.

The weather was warmer and we left Hopedale under lowering skies. We had hoped to reach Makkovik, sixty miles south, that night. However, it soon began to snow, which made visibility poor, and we ran into very rough ice. Such travel was uncomfortable and even hazardous, so we turned in toward the land, striking southwest toward Island Harbour just north of Kaipokak Bay. Later the snow was replaced by a steady drizzle, which made conditions even worse.

After a few rough hours, we reached the little settlement of Island Harbour, home of the McNeils, the Lyalls and the Alder Fords. The ancestors of the McNeils and Lyalls had come to Labrador from one of the isles of Scotland. They are a hardy breed who have contributed much to the communities in which they settled. This is especially true of the Lyalls, who have spread right across the north in the service of the RCMP and the Hudson's Bay Company.

Jim McNeil was the elder statesman of Island Harbour. Early in the second world war he and his two eldest sons had gone as usual to their trapping grounds in the interior. In their first tilt they found the dead bodies of two flyers, who had taken refuge there after crashing on a flight to Goose Bay. Taking hope from the notes scribbled on the walls, which gave the dates of the trappers' arrival at the camp in earlier years, the flyers had settled in to wait. To men unequipped for winter travel and lost in unfamiliar country, this could have been a wise choice, but instead it was tragic. This year, exceptionally poor weather delayed the McNeils; when they arrived the flyers had been dead for some time. The diary found with the bodies recounted their gradual loss of strength and their dwindling hope.

This discovery was a great shock to Jim, who could not forget that if he had left for his trapping grounds at the usual time he might have saved these men, who had bet their lives on his arrival. In later months, neither Jim nor his sons received more than passing mention from authorities for the time and effort they put into recovering the dead men's bodies and their effects.

Our stay at Island Harbour was marred by two days of pouring rain, which dampened what might have been a delightful visit in this idyllic spot. However, our hosts made us comfortable and we enjoyed the company.

The third morning was foggy, but we decided to push on to Makkovik, accompanied by Alder Ford, who needed supplies and offered to serve as our guide. Striking out from Island Harbour we were crossing the mouth of Kaipokak Bay when the fog settled upon us like a damp, deep blanket. Soon we could see only the stern of Alder's *komatik* just beyond the nose of our lead dog. Presently I noticed that the wind, which had been on my left shoulder, was now in my face. When I called my driver's attention to this, he said the wind must have shifted. I wasn't satisfied, and consulted my pocket compass. According to this, we were headed east, toward the edge of the ice, the *sina*.

After consulting Alder, we changed course and eventually arrived at Ben's Cove, the home of the Evans family. The fog had lifted by the time we had some tea, so we set off across Ben's Cove Neck to Makkovik. The neck, or portage, is notoriously difficult, with a large pond near its northern end and a steep descent to Makkovik at the other. We climbed the slope from the Evans home and as we tipped up over the rise we were disheartened by the look of the pond before us.

After days of fog and rain, the ice did not look safe. In spots it was a sickly green shading into a darker green and then into black. Alder Ford, our guide, had dropped some distance behind us when we left the Evans house. Now Bob, instead of waiting, decided to walk ahead of our dogs to search out a safe route across the ice. Doris was alarmed. I tried to reassure her with a confidence I didn't really feel, as we nervously followed Bob out onto the ice. Ben and I sat one on each side of the *komatik*, with Doris in the box between. All went well until we were about forty yards from the far shore when the dogs suddenly bolted for the nearest point of land.

The *komatik* lurched as one runner broke through weak ice. I jumped off to right it, while Ben on his side did the same. Both of us plunged into water as the whole expanse of ice beneath us collapsed. The dogs and the *komatik* followed. Luckily the water was only waist deep, but as it swirled into the *komatik* box I was afraid that Doris would soon be as drenched as the rest of us.

Bob had safely reached the shore now. As he called to his dogs, Ben and I held the *komatik* upright and managed to work our way through the water and ice to join him on the bank. We were desperately cold. Doris, sitting in the coach box in a seal skin sleeping bag, was not even damp, though the blankets beneath her bag were soggy.

Alder had not followed us but had gone safely ashore. Fortunately, he was carrying some of our load and our spare clothes. Ben and I stripped down on the edge of the pond, dried ourselves and donned dry socks, long johns, trousers and boots. We moved on through the dense woods along the trail cut across Ben's Cove Neck many years before.

At one point we had to cross a rushing stream. Someone who had travelled ahead of us not long before had built a bridge of felled trees across the torrent. Bob and Ben manouevered the *komatik* across the bridge while I followed. Halfway across, I slipped between the logs and plunged into the stream, getting drenched all over again. By the time I got out there was no point in changing again, even if I'd had any dry clothes left, for it was now pouring rain.

We negotiated the long, steep slide down the southern slope without difficulty. I remembered a calamitous experience at this same site five years earlier, travelling with Bob's eldest brother Willie. The *komatik*, shoed with bone for easier sliding in the spring, had gotten away from him. It careened down the slope and totally destroyed itself when it smashed into a tree at the bottom.

We reached Makkovik a short time later, with almost everything about us totally soaked. When we had changed and hung wet blankets and sleeping bags up to dry, we inspected the contents of our grub box. The bread was soggy and two packets of macaroni had split and swollen, forming sticky cables which clung to everything in the box.

The missionary here was George Harp, an Englishman from Lancashire, whose wife Linda came from my home town of Bristol. Both spoke excellent Inuktut. George, who was only about five feet tall, was an exceptionally versatile and capable man. It was he who, with the help of Hayward Haynes, had amputated an arm mangled beyond hope in the little village of Hebron some years before. Among his many other gifts, George was a ventriloquist and a story-teller of no mean ability. Linda was a quiet, practical lady who constantly feigned shock at his antics. We spent a couple of days at Makkovik, on one of which we inspected a Boy Scout camp set up in the woods especially for our visit. I had started Boy Scout and Wolf Cub groups there in 1938. Doris wrote of Makkovik:

> Yesterday we went all around the village in the morning visiting the people. Everybody thought Bill was very fat and healthy, and most of them gave me credit for the change. Nearly all the people here are settlers and it is more like an English village than anything else. There are many more trees here than anywhere else on the coast and it is very, very pretty. Yesterday afternoon Mr. and Mrs. Sach were out at a difficult maternity case so I went down to the school and had a look around. This school is not equipped half as well as the Nain school and teaching must be far more difficult in some ways. I don't know what will happen next year when Mrs. Rhodes (the principal) goes home.

Our return to Hopedale was uneventful, but the trip from Hopedale to Nain gave Doris a chance to witness, for the first time, a seal hunt on the ice. We were accompanied this time by Jerry Sillitt and Boas Boase of Hopedale. When one of them spotted a seal basking on the spring ice, Jerry took up his gun and *talluk*, a white screen behind which a hunter may stalk wary seals. Crawling on his belly, freezing whenever the seal raised its head, Jerry manuoevered close enough for a

shot. With the seal resting at the edge of its hole he only had time for one, but one was all he needed.

I was glad Doris got this insight into the patience and skill of Inuit hunters, but the seal delayed us somewhat; we had a cold journey in the dark through Davis Inlet Run to the Hudson's Bay post and the warm hospitality of the Butts.

Ama and Danny had rejoined us at Hopedale and were now anxious to get home, so early the next morning we set off for Boat Harbour, where we spent the night with Chesley and Mary Ford. The following day we made an easy trip back to Nain.

After a day's rest we set off again, this time north to Hebron. Ama and Danny had no wish to travel farther so we hired Martin Martin as our driver. He took Sam Brown as his assistant. On these long trips my job was to help where needed, but especially to look after my wife. I faced this trip with a little trepidation, as I had not been north of Webb's Bay with Doris before. She was not troubled by stories of the rugged journey across the Kiglapait and Kaumajet Mountains, of the vast depths of snow which accumulate in Korokuluk on the north side of the Kiglapaits, and of the difficulties of Manowa Brook on the southern slopes.

On the first leg of this trip my concern was unfounded. We made a very quick journey across the mountains to Udlik, which means "bird's nest." The name is apt, for Udlik nestles beneath a low hill and seems to be the home of countless ptarmigan. Here at the house of Joe and Paulina Mille we enjoyed a delicious meal of caribou steaks and fresh bread cooked by Sara, the Mille's "maid." (It was the custom that the daughter of a poor family would live with a more prosperous family. Her employers paid no wages but sometimes gave gifts of food to her family.) Later, after Paulina's death, Joe married Sara.

The next day we continued to Nutak, where we stayed at the Hudson's Bay Company house. Herman Leaman, the manager at Nutak, had earlier served as assistant manager at Nain, where I had married him to Sally Webb, a local girl. We spent some time as well with Sam Lyall, then the company's interpreter at Nutak, and his wife Bella. They are another of the north's amazing couples. Sam, slow of speech and very quiet, was exceptionally strong and an excellent dog driver. He served as interpreter for the Bay and the government for many years. Bella, a most remarkable woman, has left her mark of community service on Hebron, Nutak and Nain. She is an extraordinary cook, and I never saw her untidy or ruffled no matter what the crisis.

Our journey north from Nutak lay across the Kaumajat Mountains, up through the winding Itibliasuk Brook. The long, slow ascent reaches a height of almost two thousand feet, and took us more than an hour. The descent on the north side is steep and swift, and took only a few hair-raising minutes. The dogs raced down the slope with amazing speed, while Sam and Martin on either side of the *komatik* dug in their heels to slow and control our descent. In this they had help from the *spansel*, a walrus hide and chain device used to drag and slow the sled. Despite this, we fairly flew, leaving the dogs behind. Halfway down the slope was a great boulder surrounded by a very deep hole. We barely missed it.

The weather became bitterly cold when we reached sea level and made our way north across the ice of Napaktok Bay. This is the most northerly bay on the Atlantic coast in which spruce woods are found. Stunted black spruce, hardiest of trees, form the leading edge of the boreal forest across the breadth of Canada, standing in the face of Arctic gales. The last patch of forest here was almost thirty miles from Hebron but served as the chief source of fuel for the people there. In the depths of winter it would usually take them two days to cut enough firewood to load an eighteen-foot *komatik* and haul it home. Because of this the Hebronemiut often resorted to burning seal blubber in their wood stoves. This was not only very dirty but a waste of a precious "cash crop" which could be sold or traded for food. The stores bought blubber, extracted the oil and shipped it out to Newfoundland, where it was used in the manufacture of soap and, I believe, margarine.

On the north side of Napartok Bay we caught up with my colleague the Reverend Fred Grubb, returning from a visit to his parishioners in the south. We joined him for the remainder of the journey and spent two days with Fred and his wife Emily in Hebron before we turned back.

The return journey was largely uneventful. The nineteen-hour trip to Nutak on the first day was wearying and extremely cold, with a strong west wind. Doris, though huddled in blankets and a seal skin sleeping bag, suffered badly. On the last day, descending Manowa Brook, we saw again an Arctic owl which lazily spread its tremendous wings and flew away across the hills at our approach.

We had been gone thirty days and had travelled more than 750 miles. I was very proud of my young wife, who had taken every discomfort in her stride. We had other long *komatik* journeys together, and on one occasion we were lost for several hours in fog and rough ice outside of Kaipokak Bay, but Doris met everything with a cheery optimism which, I am sure, was more than she sometimes felt.

In 1945, the year after our daughter was born, I had another memorable trip to Hebron. This one included nine days lost in the Kiglapaits and ten nights in a snowhouse.

My friend and driver, Martin Martin, and I set out just after Easter. Travelling conditions were excellent and we left Nain early in the morning at a spanking pace. I had told Doris I would send her a radio message from Nutak, probably the following day. Near the entrance to Manowa Brook we overtook the heavily-loaded *komatik* of Efraim Merkurarsuk and his family, six in all, who had come from Nutak to Nain for Easter. Travelling on the rocky, frozen brook, we took the lead. We made tortuous progress around the boulders and occasional holes in the ice of the brook. It was getting continually warmer, and before we left the brook it began to snow, with great white flakes parachuting lazily down. Soon the snowfall became so thick that we could not see our lead dog from the nose of the *komatik*.

We halted, and when the other *komatik* drew up our two drivers talked briefly together and decided to camp for the night. Quietly and with unhurried skill they set about building a snow house to accommodate us all. As they carved the snow blocks and set them in position, falling snow obliterated everything around us. In forty-five minutes their job was done and mine began, for it was always my task to pack soft snow into the cracks between the blocks of snow.

I became too warm and shed my caribou skin parka, the one I had bought years earlier from the drunken fur buyer, the night before my arrival in Labrador. I tossed it on the *komatik*, which the others were unloading as they carried our gear into the snow house. When I entered some time later my parka was not to be found. It was obvious what had happened; the dogs had snatched it from the sled when our backs were turned, and had eaten it. I could have been in great difficulty without it, but luckily I had made it a practice to carry a spare, blanket parka, much inferior but adequate at this season. Nevertheless I was humiliated to have been so careless.

With eight of us in the snow house, it was crowded but warm. The next day we decided to push on despite heavy snowfall, as Efraim's family now had no food. Indeed, we had fed them the night before.

We moved on through blinding snow and were soon hopelessly lost. All we knew for sure was that we were somewhere in the Kiglapaits, a mountain block about twenty miles across, stretching inland about ten miles. For the next eight days we wandered through continuous blizzard across this mountain mass, building a new snow house each night and setting out again each morning with renewed hope of seeing a landmark one of our drivers would recognize. The dogs grew hungry, for our small store of seal meat was long gone.

After breakfast on the tenth morning we were down to a single tin of corned beef, but the morning was bright and we soon found the route. Despite very deep snow and weary dogs we reached Nutak just after midday, where we rested and replenished our food.

We set out for Hebron early the next morning, driving along in fine style until we reached the Kaumajat Mountains. We had left Efraim and his family at Nutak and were once again on our own. Slowly we travelled up the Itiblersoak Valley with the spring sun pouring down upon us. The weather changed abruptly as we crested the pass and tipped down the swift descent into Akpasinak. By the time we reached sea level we were once more in blinding snow. The speed and severity of the change in weather was astonishing.

Once out on the ice we moved slowly out toward the entrance to the bay, a mile distant. When we reached the open sea ice the wind rose with biting fury. We pushed on in the teeth of a roaring blizzard. There was no shelter, and it would have been impossible to build a snow house in these conditions. Suddenly we hit land and the dogs eagerly pulled us up over the shore ice into the slight shelter offered by low hills. We kept moving.

I was sitting on the front of the *komatik*, half-sheltered by Martin. Through the whipping snow I could just dimly see the dogs and a bit of land on either side. Suddenly the dogs disappeared, the nose of the *komatik* dipped and all of us plunged into a deep hole. Nothing was broken, but it took all our strength for nearly an hour to extricate ourselves and untangle the dogs. Finally the snow eased off and the wind dropped, so that Martin could recognize our position. A few hours later we reached Inuit homes near the mouth of Napartok Bay. There were three families, each in their own home, and we were welcomed into the largest house. These people were Hebronemiut (people of Hebron) who had come here for the spring seal hunt.

Almost as soon as we were housed and our dogs fed the wind rose again, snow began falling and the blizzard resumed. For three days it continued, and it was not until the fourth day that we could get away and reach Hebron. There I spoke to a weatherman of the U.S. Air Force, which maintained a meteorological station in Hebron at that time. He told me that winds a few days before had reached 110 miles an hour, and had done considerable damage to their equipment.

Our return to Nain took six days, which was not good but was nothing to the hardships of the trip north.

It was not always on the long trips that we had trouble. Travelling within my parish, there was plenty of scope for excitement. This was a worry to Doris, who did not travel in the depth of winter. I was nearly always remote from radio communication, and when sudden storms struck she had no way to know I was still alive.

The arrival of spring in the north was always a time of great joy. The sounds of rushing rivers and the honking of geese, the sight of the land unveiled, and the appearance of the first robin stirred our hearts. Perhaps the most exciting thing was the freeing of the ocean from the deadly grip of ice. Life's tempo changed then, for spring was a time of preparation, of hope and new life, and a time when we could await news of the outside world and of loved ones far away.

It was also a time when thoughts turned to boats and a struggle against another element of this fierce land: the mighty, restless sea. When I was a small boy, fascinated by ships, I had planned to run away to sea with a young friend. We didn't go, of course, but we haunted the quays of Bristol and dreamed of foreign lands while clinging to the comfort of home. My romantic notions faded as I grew, but the sea was yet to play a large part in my life. I covered many miles in open trap boats and more in the mission launches at Nain and Makkovik.

On the whole my travel in small boats was less rigorous than travel by dog team; it was usually in the coastal schooners that I confirmed my reputation as a jinx. However, I do remember one nerve-racking trip by small boat, when weather had nothing to do with our danger and discomfort. When I was transferred from Nain to Makkovik for a year in 1938, I travelled the whole distance, nearly two hundred miles, in an open fishing boat. We bailed furiously almost the whole time.

I was travelling with Walter Dicker, a settler from Makkovik, and Josua Atsertatajok, an Inuk from the same village. Time and again we had to beach the boat and try to caulk the leaks. We made temporary repairs at Boat Harbour, Davis Inlet and Big Bay, and finally undertook major repairs at Hopedale.

This time we thought we had the problems licked, and set out with high hopes. Within twenty-five miles, at Tikkerarsuk, we had to beach the boat again. There were several Inuit families at this place, which gave me a chance to hire another boat for the scant remaining distance to Makkovik, which I reached that evening. Walter and Josua showed up a full two days later, with Josua at the tiller and Walter still furiously bailing. Their boat, condemned that fall, rejoiced in the name of *Xenia* but people called her the *Eczema*. Considering the trouble she gave, that seemed a far more fitting name.

When I returned to Nain two years later (after sixteen months in Makkovik and eight months in England, getting married and studying tropical medicine), I inherited a far more substantial craft. A thirty-six foot cabin cruiser called the *Seeko*, she had formerly belonged to the explorer, Admiral Donald MacMillan. He had sailed her from Boston to Nain and donated her to the Mission. She was designed for northern waters, built of oak and double-planked. She had a galley, a head and accommodations for four. This was a far cry from the rude comforts of an open trap boat. She was, however, a great roller and was difficult to handle in heavy seas. Doris and our daughter Stephanie and I spent many happy days and a few rough ones aboard her, visiting my parishoners in the bays and at their sealing and fishing places on the outer coast. I often used her, too, to convey sick patients from the outside places to the station. She gave the Mission good service for more than forty years.

Another mission boat, acquired from Newfoundland and brought to Makkovik by Captain Job Barbour, was the *John Cunningham*, but her service with the Mission was considerably shorter than that of the *Seeko*. She was an elegant-looking boat but not half as sturdy.

In 1941 officials of the Hudson's Bay Company flew into Nain. Their aircraft was the harbinger of great changes, not only in transportation but in the commerce of northern Labrador, for the Company was about to pull out. They had taken over the retail trade from the Moravian Mission in 1924, and like the Mission, they had lost money.

It was not until the terrible flu epidemic of the following year that aircraft became a common sight in northern Labrador. With the establishment of the Goose Air Base, mercy flights became common and both the Canadian and American airmen, especially the former, were most generous not only in flying mercy missions but in assisting missionaries and police to move about in their work.

Eastern Provincial Airways established a bush plane service in 1949, though it was confined to charter flights in the beginning. Wheeler Airways entered the scene shortly after. In the fall of 1951, a man named Eric Blackwood flew a single-engine Beechcraft into the Inuit communities. He hoped to enter provincial politics, and clearly saw this as a means of drawing attention.

The coming of aircraft transformed travel in Labrador and did much to ease a sense of isolation which was only then becoming a problem. In my early years in Labrador, we got mail three times a winter if we were lucky. We were icebound from late November until the following June or even July, if the ice pack drifting down the coast from the Arctic was especially heavy. Radio communication was poor, and in any case only the whites had radio receivers. Supplies in the stores were limited. We were too busy with our own affairs, with helping each other and keeping ourselves amused, to feel out of touch with a world so unlike our own. Even people living away from the station in very small groups never mentioned isolation.

I believe, in fact, that isolation is a state of mind, and one which had little meaning on the coast until mail order catalogues appeared. It was these more than anything in our surroundings which promoted a sense of deprivation. Their bright illustrations suggested, to a people not yet cynical about advertising, that everyone else was living a life of great ease and material plenty, pampered by comforts we lacked but had scarcely missed until then.

In 1952, for the first time, Hopedale got its mail by air. Mail for Nain and Hebron still went the rest of the way by dog team. I made complaints through our federal member, Tom Ashbourne, to the postmaster general, Alcide Cote. His reply quoted figures suggesting that it would be far too costly to fly mail to the northern communities. In my next letter I disputed this calculation, for it failed to take into account the money already being spent on the courier service by dog team. Furthermore, several of the couriers had suffered dreadfully from carrying mail in very severe conditions. Indeed two of them, an Inuk and an Indian, had died of pneumonia contracted while carrying the mail. The next mail plane went right to Hebron.

While this was the first official air mail into northern Labrador, we had actually got thirteen bags of mail at Christmas six years earlier, thanks to both confusion and generosity. Three bags of mail for the north coast were delivered by mistake to Goose Bay and missed the last boat north. When the chief operations officer of the RCAF, Squadron Leader Ted Snider heard of this, he contacted postal authorities asking permission to bring us this mail on the next mercy flight. The post office not only gave permission, but found ten more bags of mail for us at the post office in Goose Bay. So for the first time in the 174-year history of the Mission, the people of Nain received Christmas mail at Christmas, instead of the following spring. At the same time, Mr. and Mrs. Cyril Watkins, church leaders in Happy Valley, offered to provide some Christmas candy for the children of Nain if the RCAF would carry it. This gesture led to the annual Christmas Toy Drop, originally organized by the U.S. and Canadian air forces and continued by the latter. The Toy Drop, which lasted for twenty-eight years, provided every child in northern Labrador with a toy, an article of clothing and candy each Christmas.

The advent of aircraft spelled the end of my dog team travel, at least for the longer journeys. However, my reputation as a jinx endured and some pilots hesitated to carry me. In fact the notoriety grew far beyond the bounds of my parish. I received a telegram one day from a government official in St. John's, which read: AM HOPING TO TRAVEL IN LABRADOR FOR NEXT TWO WEEKS. WOULD YOU PLEASE STAY AT HOME?

The low point in my passenger career came six months before my retirement, in January, 1971. Early that month I had gone to hospital with chest pains and was informed that I had angina, a form of heart disease. Despite this, I decided to go ahead with plans to accompany my successor, the Reverend David Dickenson, on a trip to Nain the following day. Our business there was rather pressing.

We left Goose Bay at 8 a.m. in one of Labrador Airways' single-engine Otters. I sat in the co-pilot's seat, beside our pilot Tom Sims, while David sat with the other two passengers, Nancy Pamak of Nain and Bill Shiwak of Rigolet, at the back of the aircraft behind a huge load of mail. The morning was crisp and clear around Goose Bay but cloudy to the east, so we kept well inland, heading first for Hopedale.

After about an hour, our engine suddenly quit. Tom calmly fiddled some controls and got it started again. We were flying over very thick forest, about eighty miles inland from Makkovik, with no nearby ponds or clearings for an emergency landing. A few minutes later the engine quit again, and nothing would revive it. We had just crossed a lightly wooded marsh and were once again over heavy forest. Tom turned back, holding our altitude as best he could in an effort to reach the marsh.

As we glided down, it was obvious we were not going to clear some trees at the edge of the marsh. However, they were small and fragile, and we smashed right through them, plowing into deep snow in a surprisingly gentle landing. Before we came to a stop the plane tipped to its left and I thought we might flip, but the left ski hit a stump and restored our balance.

As soon as we stopped, Tom yelled, "Everybody out!" I leaped out the door on my side and landed in snow almost up to my chin. Tom was in the same state on the other side of the aircraft. So were the three rear passengers, whose door had burst open on impact. We were totally unharmed except for Tom, who had a small cut over his right eye. About three feet had been sheared off the starboard wing of the plane.

Tom climbed back into his seat and tried to make radio contact with Goose Bay. When he got nothing, we looked things over and discovered that our antenna was gone, apparently stripped off by trees in our landing. Tom set out on snowshoes and soon found it tangled in a broken tree. With the antenna restrung, we easily contacted Battle Harbour, and they relayed our distress call to Goose Bay.

There was nothing to do now but make ourselves comfortable and wait. We erected a tent along the starboard wing of the plane, got out a primus stove and began melting snow for coffee. Bill Shiwak gathered dry wood for a fire. It was snowing lightly.

Authorities in Goose Bay advised us a helicopter was not available to pick us up directly. The nearest lake where a plane could land was about five miles away. I knew my ailing heart would not stand a hike of that distance in deep snow. The alternative was for Labrador Airways to fly out a snowmobile in the Otter, to ferry us back to the pond with that.

It was now about mid-morning. The snow had stopped and it was getting colder. Our fire was burning merrily and the coffee was ready, but I didn't enjoy it much; it was full of flotsam, little bits of spruce needles and other debris from the snow we had melted to make it. We took turns with the snowshoes, tramping down snow around the plane, mostly to keep warm. We told stories, melted snow and brewed more nauseous coffee. David had with him a small pup he was delivering to a friend in Hopedale. The pup was not impressed with life in the wilderness, nor the smoke from our fire, and he whined piteously until someone picked him up.

About noon we heard the sound of a plane but it seemed to be far to the west of us. Shortly after that we heard it again, this time somewhere to the east. Tom shot off a flare, part of the plane's emergency equipment, and within fifteen minutes another single Otter was cruising above us. Its pilot was Ian Massie, son of a former Hudson's Bay company manager in Nain. Tom and Ian conferred by radio and settled the arrangements.

Ian would land at a lake to the north of us. We were to remain where we were until he and his co-pilot reached us by snowmobile. They would bring additional snowshoes, because we only had two pair. We were cheerful and confident. Five miles is nothing to a snowmobile; we should expect help within an hour, perhaps by 1:30.

Time dragged on. Dense woods and deep snow hindered our rescuers, and they did not reach us till 3:30. Ian, the chief pilot for Labrador Airways, assessed the damage to our plane and organized our trek back to the lake. There were five on snowshoes and two on the snowmobile. I was one of the latter.

I have never liked snowmobiles. Clearly they have their place in the lives of people of the north, but they always seemed to me an intruder in the silence, destroying underbrush and inflicting an urgency into the unhurried tempo of life I had known in my early days in Labrador.

On this occasion I was pleased enough to see one, but the next two hours were a nightmare. I clung to the driver as we weaved and buffetted through thick forest, lurching from side to side and sometimes sinking helplessly in the deep snow. Tom, then Ian, then his co-pilot took turns driving while I desperately hung on to each in turn, at times barely missing having a leg crushed against a tree. Before we had gone a mile I was exhausted and could hardly breathe. My heart was pounding furiously and David feared a heart attack. On one of the many times we bogged down, when I dragged myself off the machine while others heaved it up to a firm footing, I begged Ian to leave me and take the others to safety. I was feeling desperately afraid that I would never see the rescue plane, and that I was hindering the progress of the others. Although I have many times been in trouble in the wilderness I have never been as anxious as I was then. I must admit, though, that I was relieved when my suggestion was laughed off. Ian assured me we would soon make it.

It was long past dark when we came out on the lake. Ian had to seek permission to fly in the dark, because a single Otter can normally fly only in daylight. He got permission, of course. Before we took off we saw the lights of a plane overhead. We learned later that Ian's colleagues in Goose Bay were alarmed by his long radio silence and had come out to look for us.

We boarded our rescue plane, which was desperately cold. It was also difficult to start, and when it finally started we were still stuck. Water had seeped out under the snow on the ice and our skis had frozen in. Here again the skidoo came in useful and our crew knew exactly what to do. They cut two long trees from the adjacent forest, and two men used these to pry our skis and wheels free while the third man beat a pathway down the lake for our take-off. After much effort we got airborne, and landed in Goose Bay some twelve hours after our crash landing. Although I felt alright that evening, I was quite unable to walk the following day. Every movement of my shoulders was excruciating. However, in a few days I was feeling well enough to resume work.

As far as I know the cause of our engine failure was never discovered. A party of engineers flew in to repair the damaged wing, and woodsmen cut out a runway for the take-off. Ian Massie went back to fly the damaged Otter to Goose Bay, and found he could not achieve much altitude. Later he flew her back to the DeHavilland workshops for an overhaul before she resumed service with the Labrador Airways fleet.

My experiences at sea, on ice and in the air have added to the admiration I feel for my travelling companions, both white and Inuit. The latter always made me envious of their skill. I never ceased to wonder at their patience and calmness in any situation. From the whites I learned of a fellowship among travellers in the north which cannot be matched in more civilized places. Cars, for example, isolate their drivers from each other. They become instruments of competition between people jockeying for position. Travellers by small boat and dog team are continually watching out for each other, alert for signs of difficulty, willing and sometimes anxious to stop and chat, to exchange news of families and advice on travel conditions.

My memories of dog team travel are tinged with sadness, because those days are gone. Where once a man depended entirely on these magnificent northern huskies, today he has replaced them with a snowmobile. It is true that the dogs were great thieves and gluttons, but they were dependable and they had a sense of direction. A man might find shelter and warmth among them, and sometimes they offered a devotion which was amazing in half-tamed animals. In times of starvation people might even eat a dog, however unwillingly, and many have.

But a snowmobile? This is a noisy, stinking, untrustworthy and even dangerous substitute for dogs. In wooded country it destroys trees and bushes. It drives away the game. On rough ice it can physically damage its driver. It is expensive to buy and expensive to maintain, and it pollutes the land and air.

It was true that dogs could become killers, but this was usually due to carelessness on the part of the owner or the victim. The snowmobile, too, is a killer of the careless. It can get a man into trouble faster than he can get out of it, or break down at some hopeless distance from shelter or safety. The speed and the roar of these machines can dull the senses and lead the unwary onto bad ice a dog would avoid. Indeed I am told that drownings and death by exposure when snowmobiles break through bad ice are now a leading cause of accidental death on the Labrador coast.

So I say, give me dogs and slow journeys over speed and discomfort. I shall always feel a special affection for the husky.

13

NORTHERN SPRING

It is only within the last thirty or forty years that the Arctic and sub-Arctic have come to the attention of politicians, economists and ecologists. The "northern wastes" were once regarded as fit only for nomadic Inuit and polar bears. Perhaps it was the Russians, reaching out toward the northern parts of their country, who shamed us into some attention to our own. In any case, during and after World War II our Arctic became important not only as part of the defensive perimeter of the Free World but because air travel across the North provides the shortest route between Europe and North America.

With the growing importance of the North there has appeared a spate of books by people who have spent a lifetime or a season or even just a few days in the Arctic. People "outside" are showing an increasing interest in the lives of northerners and in the commercial resources of northern regions. Tours of the Arctic are now a regular feature of travel agents' literature. However, there is no need to travel to the icebound shores of the Far North to sample the flavour of Arctic life. Labrador can provide these adventures, thrills, joys and miseries in ample measure.

While the severity of a northern winter seems to fascinate those who enjoy central heating in southern communities, northern residents take the winter blizzards, the intense cold and the problems of travel and isolation in their stride. There is a thrill in the challenge of winter, but it is the northern spring which offers more.

Before the thaw, in mid-March or April, snow buntings arrive, the first visitors from the south. At first they appear in small flocks, perhaps half a dozen at a time. Then, usually following a heavy fall of snow, more arrive in flocks of hundreds. They are followed by the hawks, hovering lazily over woodlands watching for careless mice which venture up from their snowbound tunnels to the dazzling surface. By the end of April there is the wonderful smell of good, bare earth, appearing now where winter gales had swept the ground almost clear. By this time, too, the first of the lapland longspurs, chestnut-headed strangers, appear among the flocks of snow buntings still streaming north.

On the hillsides beyond the villages, plants are springing into life and the scent of the tiny flowers of the blackberry (*Empetrum nigrum*) fills the air. Then come the robins: only a few at first, then dozens. With the small birds comes the destroyer, the butcher bird or northern shrike. As rivers break up the Canada geese arrive, trumpeting their stately way north. Offshore, eider ducks and gulls are already nesting, and they are followed by black ducks, guillemots, mergansers, murres and other large birds.

Among the smaller birds are the beautiful myrtle warblers, juncos, ruby-crowned kinglets and a host of others. Walking along the shore one may see a curious dance: the semi-palmated plover seeking to entice the intruder from the vicinity of its nest. It never worked with me; the performance announced the presence of a nest, and I would search till I found it, enjoying the dance the whole while.

There is an astonishing variety of plant life, most of it hugging the ground. Dwarf rhododendrons, tiny azaleas, ledum, diapensias, saxifrages and vetches are among the dainty flowers which adorn the land in spring. Many species of willow creep over the ground, displaying catkins of vivid hues.

There are still large patches of snow on the hills, many of which will remain until early summer. But the sea ice, the winter highway, airstrip and playground of Labrador villages, gradually yields to the eroding influence of sun, wind and fog.

To the Inuit and settlers, spring means rest from the struggles of winter, and preparations for the bounty of cod, salmon, Arctic char and other fish. On beautiful spring mornings the Inuit greet us with broad smiles and the word *sillaki*, which means "wonderful day." From a settler, the greeting might be, "Fierce pretty day, sir." Or, as an old fellow said to me on a glorious morning, "It's wonderful in the spring when the little birds is bawling and the brooks is a-brooking."

So it is, when the fierce winter has spent itself and the land and people are reborn.

Doris wrote of one splendid spring holiday in 1943, a few months after the epidemic.

After all the anxiety and work this spring I was anxious to get some sort of break, even if it was only for a couple of days. The opportunity came when Clara's father, Amos Voisey, started bringing down lumber. Clara and I both packed very hurriedly on a rainy morning and set off for Voisey's Bay in an open motor boat with Clara's two brothers.

It was calm but grey, and we were very cold after eight hours in the boat. We were never on the open sea but always skirting down between islands, through tickles where there are strong tidal currents or "rattles," or across wide bays where the wind was cold and the lop made the boat roll a little. We stopped at one house for a cup of tea and then went the long trip up the wide bay to where Clara's home is sheltered in a snug little harbour surrounded by smooth, wave-washed islands. Everywhere we saw the black heads of seals popping out of the water, and flocks of water birds, startled at the sound of the engine, hurried away in very tidy formation. Bottle-nose divers, small, black, duck-like birds were most numerous, and black and white sea pigeons skimmed up off the water near most of the islands. Between Nain and Karmarsuk, where we stopped for our cup of tea, there are said to be over two hundred islands!

I was very glad to get to bed that first night. I slept well and awoke to a gloriously bright Saturday morning. Uncle Amos had promised to take us to the seal nets on the other side of the bay if the weather was good, and I persuaded Aunt Emma to come too.

It was warm, and calm on the water. There were flocks of birds everywhere and hundreds of sea gulls were feeding from the wave-swept, smooth rocks along the coast . . . . The motor boat stopped just above the seal net, which is very much like the salmon nets in the Severn, except that it is much stronger and anchored out in the water . . . .

It was terribly exciting for me when they hauled the first seal. It was a great big harp, about six feet long and all tangled in the net. The two men unravelled the worst tangles and then with the gunwhale of their small boat level with the water they hauled the seal aboard and finished untangling the net and mending the holes before going on to the next seal. The weight of the dead seals dragged the net well below the surface and not even the corks were showing. There were ten seals altogether. The men hauled four into the small boat and lashed the others to the sides, then later hauled them aboard the motor boat . . . .

Clara and I were watching the sun set, sitting on an island at low water on Saturday evening when a whole school of seals came up out of the water, just below us, to breathe. We could see the white of their tummies as they came up on their backs before they popped their heads out of the water. It was a very still evening with only a slight rippling on the water, and suddenly it sounded as though a number of small steam engines had started to puff. It took me quite a while to realize that the odd sound was the breathing of the seals. Sunday dawned another glorious day and there was much mysterious activity around the house during the morning, and then I was asked if I would like to go for a picnic. All the young people came and we went in the motor boat across the bay and visited all the smaller islands.

The first was small and rather rocky but there were a few patches of turf and one pond. The pond looked exactly like one from an English farmyard. It was quite green and surrounded with short-cropped grass bespeckled with duck droppings and occasional feathers. It was here, in a nest sheltered by a ledge of rock and lined with chocolate-coloured down that I found my first duck eggs: pale green in colour and about twice the size of hen's eggs. I had no qualms in taking them because the whole scene seemed to be so thoroughly domesticated . . . I might not have found the nest if the mother had not flown up so conveniently and shown me where to go. Most of the nests had five or six eggs, but mine had only four. We found twenty-six eggs on this island, a half of our complete haul. The other islands were bigger and the nests were much more difficult to find.

A tiny semi-palmated plover attracted our attention by its peculiar behaviour. It ran around in circles and flopped its wings and its tail on the rocks, peeping at us in a most ludicrous fashion. As followed, it became more and more excited. If we went to walk away it followed us with its wings spread trying its uttermost to regain our attention. All this fuss was because it had a wee nest with four speckled eggs in it. We might easily have walked on it, the camouflage was so good. In fact, if you looked away you had to search to find the nest again.

The most exciting thing I saw during the afternoon was a goose sitting on her nest. She was on a ledge of rock only a few feet below me. Bob got within a couple of feet of her before she flew from the nest, honking her loudest. She had hardly flown when the gander flew up from a ledge below and they both landed on the sea and swam away from us, shouting their indignation as they went. (The next day we had gander for dinner but it was very tough.)

Breakfast Point was the spot we chose for our picnic. Jim went off with the kettle to find water, Clara unpacked the haversack, and Kitty boiled some duck eggs in sea water after Bob had got the fire going. Rose and I gathered fuel and when the water boiled Kitty cooked some smoked trout (Arctic char) and we had a grand meal.

14

HUSKIES

The huskies that roamed our Labrador villages were at once crafty and stupid, ferocious and docile—a catalogue of contradictions. The husky had remarkable endurance, yet could be incredibly lazy. He could be courageous and sturdy, bold enough to attack a polar bear, but would sometimes display the most abject cowardice. He could be trustworthy and friendly at one moment, yet become savage in the blink of an eye. To watch a team of huskies being fed was to witness brutal combat; they would snarl, snap, bite and claw every animal in reach. They would eat almost anything, but they could go on working for days without eating at all. They could haul extraordinary loads all day, at an average speed of about four miles an hour.

One of my drivers once sold a good, peaceful dog to a Mountie and was dismayed to learn, a few days later, that the Mountie had had to shoot the animal. It simply would not acknowledge its new master's right even to harness it.

Huskies would sometimes attack humans, but in nearly every case some careless action triggered the dog's ferocity, which lay just beneath the surface. Among the Inuit and settlers it was an unwritten law that dogs which had bitten humans should be destroyed.

The Inuit did not pamper their dogs and indeed were sometimes brutal with them. Nothing else would get their attention when they fought. During the summer, many of the teams would be left to roam wild on an island, scavenging the shores. At such times they became wary and shy.

Labrador huskies were apparently first used to carry individual packs; only later were they used to pull sleds. Until comparatively recent times they were also used in hunting polar bears, holding the quarry at bay until the hunter could dispatch it with spear or rifle.

Huskies suffer most of the same diseases which afflict dogs in other latitudes. The most common and serious is distemper, which seems to appear in six or seven-year cycles. Distemper can decimate the dog population, leaving only a few alive. The survivors produce a new and powerful strain of dogs which go unchallenged by disease until the next epidemic, when the weaker huskies again die off. One epidemic was so severe that I appealed to the government for help, because the dogs were vital to the livelihood of our people. A government veterinarian arrived, innoculated half a dozen dogs in Nain and departed, leaving his supplies with us. My colleagues and I treated numerous dogs that summer; I innoculated about six hundred in the Nain area myself.

During this epidemic, I realized that the apparent cruelty of the Inuit toward their dogs was not the whole picture. The harshness hid a great solicitude, for the animals were central to the economy of each household, hauling firewood and water, moving families to their camps, carrying men to the hunting grounds and hauling the meat home. Only in times of absolute starvation would the Inuit eat dog meat, but in such times the dogs were a kind of insurance.

Until the coming of light aircraft to northern Labrador some thirty years ago, dogs were the only means of transport in winter. Yet air transport is expensive and it was not until the arrival of snowmobiles (universally called "skidoos", regardless of the brand) that the dogs began to lose their prominence in the life of Labrador. Today they have been almost entirely displaced. With them have gone the skills of their drivers.

Driving a team of seven or eight dogs called for great ability and patience. Sometimes the going was so easy that the driver had nothing to do; but when there was deep snow, rough ice or obstacles on the portage trail the driver and his dogs could struggle to the limit of their endurance. At these times the Inuit, who have practically no expletives in their own language, would draw heavily on English. Even those who knew very little English were well supplied for times like these.

The gradual disappearance of the husky is, in my opinion, a sad aspect of the changing way of life in the north. Perhaps skidoos are more efficient, and they are certainly faster, but they are noisy, stinking machines with no soul. How different from the huskies! Noisy they are too, indeed, but they have character and, I am sure, souls. They display affection and trust and they will work till they drop.

15

A NORTHERN GOURMET

Carving by Ray Hunter

I suppose there are few who would associate the Arctic and sub-Arctic with delectable meals. Yet the Inuit are as fond of food and as particular in its preparation as anyone else. Some of their dishes would tickle the palate of the most sophisticated patrons of fine restaurants. Yet there are many outsiders living in the north who miss the true value and uniqueness of native foods because they "eat with their eyes."

The first meal I ate when I arrived in Hopedale in 1935 was seal meat. When the dark meat was placed before me my stomach heaved slightly, but I was hungry and I got it down. Over the years I acquired a taste for this very rich, vitamin-filled meat, the staple of nearly everyone's diet.

We depended almost entirely on wild meat, and would eat nearly any game with satisfaction after a time of scarcity. Seal, caribou, porcupine, Arctic hare, white whales, walrus, porpoise and bear, as well as a wide variety of sea birds, were available, as were numerous species of fish. Many of these would be classed as luxuries if they were available at all outside the north.

For whites, the quality of a meal depended chiefly on the cooking, but the Inuit could eat meat, especially seal meat, frozen, dried, occasionally raw or even putrified. Indeed a classic dish was seal meat putrified by slow heat or burial. Another formidable dish was seal blubber mixed with redberries and the roe of Arctic char, topped with fermented seal oil. Another was seal intestines and their contents, mixed with seal blood. My queasy stomach could not handle these, but no gourmet could wish for a more tasty and delightful meal than slowly-fried seal liver. Seal brains, coated with oatmeal and lightly fried, are another treat I can vouch for. Very little of the precious seal carcass went to waste in Inuit homes; what humans could not eat the ravenous dogs would eat gladly.

Caribou gave many varied and delicious meals, equally welcome to Inuit and white. Having been raised in England, where venison is a treat reserved to the aristocracy, I found caribou one of the finest meats I have ever tasted. Roasted, fried or broiled, it makes little difference. Caribou is magnificent food.

The Hettasch's, our predecessors at Nain, showed us how to make caribou sausage. We put the venison through a grinder, added a little well-minced fat back pork and spices, then a little wine, then put the mixture through the grinder once again. This time, as it emerged from the spout we packed it into tubes of well-cleaned and salted bear gut. We tied the tubes off at intervals and hung them for a week to ten days in the smoke house, slowly curing over a smouldering fire of crowberry heath (*Empetrum negrum*). The finished sausage was fit for princes.

Caribou heart, like seal's heart, made a splendid meal. Caribou tongue was rich and excellent eating, superior in every way to seal tongue, which was not to be spurned either.

The Inuit would often eat the stomach of the caribou with its contents, a silver-coloured moss, as soon as the animal was killed. They also ate the eyes, swallowed whole as whites eat oysters. My friend the late Pa Perrett told of being treated at one settler home with caribou eye pie!

As with the seal, little of the caribou was wasted. The skins were prized for clothing and bed robes, and as babiche for snowshoes. Only the liver is discarded because there have been times when, eaten raw, it has caused illness. This may be due to an excess of Vitamin A.

I remember one of my earliest meals in Hopedale, which tasted remarkably like veal. However, calves in Hopedale were as scarce as penguins. When I had finished my host asked, "How did you enjoy the pussy cat?" I nearly choked, and felt the revolt rising in my stomach. "Yes," he continued, "mountain cat. Some people call them lynx." I had to confess that I found it delicious, and I have learned since that many Labrador folk praise it highly.

Many also enjoy the distinctive flavour of eider ducks, sea pigeons and a variety of other sea birds which nest or migrate along the

Labrador coast and which, in their season, provide much of the local diet. I myself never enjoyed the somewhat fishy flavour of these birds, though I found them more palatable if they were skinned before cooking.

The eggs of sea birds were another matter. After a winter of eggs shipped from Newfoundland in October, already stale when we got them, fresh eggs from the colonies of sea birds were one of the many delights of spring. Not only did they provide fresh food and welcome protein, but we used them in baking cakes and biscuits. The Inuit could eat prodigious numbers of eggs at one sitting, and enjoyed them all the more if the embryo was well begun. Those days are gone. Unfeeling governments have banded together to prohibit this harvest, protecting these birds for later destruction by sports hunters in the south. The number of eggs taken locally was such a tiny fraction of the total, it is difficult to believe such measures could be justified on the grounds of conservation alone. It is equally questionable what right government has to prohibit a practice begun centuries before the coming of white men.

The polar bear, too, is now a protected species, but with more reason. In any case I found its meat not at all to my liking, though I might have come to like it, as I did seal, if it had been available more often. Young black bear, however, is very palatable.

We enjoyed an abundance of fish, of course. The king of the plate was surely Arctic char, a delectable fish. Smoked, steamed, fried, baked, stuffed, boiled or even raw, char provided the finest of sea food. In former times Inuit speared them in the rivers, but by my time they were taken mostly in nets. Often as soon as the char was out of the net an Inuit fisherman would suck out and swallow the eyes. They often preserved their char as *pipse*, made by lightly salting fillets held together only by the skin of the tail, and hanging them over racks to cure in the sun. Deep slashes in the flesh helped to promote even drying. Rows of drying *pipse*, a startling vivid red, brightened the fishing camps in July and August.

As a closing note to this chapter I recall a visit of the Duke of Edinburgh's Commonwealth Study Group to the Goose Bay area. The party included men from all parts of the Commonwealth. Several men from my church had the pleasure of entertaining this group, and our discussions ranged across a great many subjects including, of course, food. Our visitors were fascinated and questioned us at length about native customs and foods.

A gentleman from India turned to Titus, an Inuk, and said, "I understand that you people eat your meat raw."

Titus wagged his finger and replied with great dignity, "We do not eat our meat raw, we eat it frozen." This was not absolutely true, but it made a useful distinction.

16

SOME OF
MY RELIGION

My years of contact with the Inuit and settlers of northern Labrador did more to mature my faith and to help me understand the problems of faith than anything else in my life. Their simplicity, sincerity and trust in the mercy and love of God were an inspiration. They helped me to see that faith and religion were not matters of black and white or positive and negative. They understood that religion can make demands which strain faith to its utmost.

At such times the Inuit would say *ajornarmat*, which meant that it cannot be helped. They accepted poverty and other hardships and tragedies with fatalism and without the least resentment, but with an innocence I found astounding. They would accept the poverty of others, too, as the result of misfortune, never of the man's laziness or his wife's ineptness or the irresponsibility of both.

We ourselves were poor financially because Moravian missionaries are poorly paid. I found it difficult to accept that we had so little and were expected to give so much, though I knew that by comparison with our Inuit parishioners we were well off. We learned, however, that we had riches far beyond earthly possessions, riches which could not be taken from us but which we might squander if we ceased to care about each other and our people. Having said that, I want to discuss my faith and the demands it makes on me.

I could never believe that all men are born equal. To me the inequalities of life are so manifest that to declare equality is laughable.

I do believe, however, that in the sight of God all humans have equal value, so that as Christians we cannot permit inequalities of education or opportunity. Everyone should have an equal chance to make the best possible life, and a job with a living wage should be every man's right.

I believe that a person should be judged on the basis of what he has accomplished with the opportunities and talents he has. Money and social position are of no consequence. I believe that the true wealth of a nation lies in the potential of its people for good, and that the quality of a life is determined by an individual's spiritual values and inner peace.

From my earliest days I was taught that compassion and courtesy must be a vital part of my religion. Compassion for the underprivileged, for victims of circumstance, for the sick, infirm and the aged, is widely praised. Compassion for the morally weak, the loveless and wayward, has sometimes led to my being criticized for "weakness" in responding to the mistakes of my parishioners. This has never worried me for I have never agreed to a lowering of moral standards; I merely tried to show a compassion and understanding often lacking in organized religion.

This is evident in the issue of divorce and remarriage. The refusal to bless a genuine effort to amend a mistake and start again is, in my opinion, a cold-blooded and loveless response to a problem which calls for sympathy, understanding and guidance. Similarly the refusal to baptise "illegitimate" children is an act of callous men.

I want to explain a tradition of "church discipline," the abandonment of which I believe has harmed the integrity of community life in northern Labrador. I have already explained in an earlier chapter how the chapel servants and village elders formed a council called the *AngajoKauKattiget* which maintained harmony in the villages for generations, regulating the conduct of hunting and the sharing or loaning of equipment and houses, and curbing personal misconduct where it threatened social order. One of the ultimate measures of control was church discipline, in which someone guilty of a severe breach of community standards was denied Communion until he showed genuine repentence. In a church which confined the celebration of Holy Communion to five times a year, to keep it a special event in the life of the community, this exclusion was a painful measure. With a few exceptions, no person could be put in this position on the evidence of others. Only a private confession to the missionary or to one of the elders could result in placing a delinquent church member under discipline. When I became superintendent in 1941 I placed even more onus on the offender; only he, after discussion and prayers with the missionary or one of the elders, could decide if discipline was warranted. I believe I proved this was a more effective way of dealing with those who felt a need to confess, though some of the Inuit and my clerical brethren accused me of being "soft."

There were missionaries who saw no point in this form of confession, and there have been some whose lack of fluency in Inuktut made pastoral counselling difficult. So it was that after my retirement in 1971, and the retirement of another bilingual colleague, the practice of confession and church discipline was abandoned. I still believe this was a mistake.

The old system of confession, or "speaking," was an outlet for pent-up emotions and guilt, while discipline offered a sense of atonement. The Inuit looked upon the missionary as one with whom they could share the burden of their feelings, one who could point them to God and show them how to mend their ways and adapt to the pressures upon them. With this outlet gone, the burden of guilt and confusion can be heavy indeed, and may lead to depression and despair.

In our dealings with our parishioners we had to remember that even the most unloveable characters were God's children. It was so easy to work with, love and serve the smiling, faithful, responsive and friendly members of the congregation. With the unloved and seemingly unloveable it was a different matter; we had to remind ourselves that those who were dirty, lazy, slatternly and even evil needed our help more than those who were loveable and faithful. In time, as love widened and understanding grew, it was not so difficult to feel an affection even for these. We learned not to condemn them because we had not stood where they stood and could not really appreciate the difficulties and the pressures they endured. How can anyone profess to love God if he does not love his fellows?

Finally I believe that Jesus Christ alone is Head of His Church. Christ's authority is above all denominations and church leaders. This is the central teaching of the Moravian Brethren's Church (*Unitas Fratrum*), whose motto is, "Our Lamb has conquered; let us follow Him."

Happy Valley 1970

17

RETROSPECT

In 1957, after 186 years of operating out of Nain, mission headquarters were moved to Happy Valley. This was done both to improve service to central Labrador, where many coastal residents had moved after construction of a major air base during the war, and to take advantage of the airport for easier contact with England and Newfoundland.

After twenty-two years on the north coast, I prepared for the move with very mixed feelings. The people of Nain were not only parishioners but friends with whom we had shared joy and sorrow, want and plenty. However, I did feel that I could work more effectively on behalf of the Inuit and settlers from a less remote location.

In our years on the coast I had struggled to combat the paternalism which too often infects our dealings with native people. While their heritage was something they and all Canadians should cherish, I felt that the Inuit should have every chance to choose their future and should therefore have access to the education which makes these choices possible. Our radio station and newspaper were part of this, giving an outlet for the views of Inuit and settler alike, expanding their perception of the world beyond the coast.

The base of democratic government of the church and the community had grown during my time on the coast. Women now had a voice in local affairs as well as in church policy, and congregations had more responsibility for moral conduct within the community. The education system had been much improved, and many had worked together to reinforce the local economy.

I believed, as I left Nain, that I was leaving a people much more capable of expressing themselves than before. They had surely strengthened my own Christian beliefs and faith. I hoped I had demonstrated that missionaries were not remote figures quick to condemn, but were motivated by love of Christ and their fellows.

Many have accused missionaries of having had a repressive influence over otherwise joyful, carefree native peoples. Doubtless some have had this effect, and some perhaps in Labrador, but my own experience has been that most sought to bring better and happier conditions to the Inuit and settlers.

It is true that until 1942 church rules did not permit dancing or playing cards. I felt that both these rules were wrong. I do not dance myself, lacking much of a sense of rhythm, but I have always felt that dancing is a way of expressing joy. Soon after I became superintendent I proposed that we discard this rule, which people were ignoring anyway. I was not surprised to see this motion pass without dissent, but I expected a more vigorous defence of the rule against cards. However this, too, was deleted from the church rules.

The use of alcohol was another matter. Church rules did not explicitly forbid drinking, and in fact in the earliest days missionaries had brewed their own "small beer" as it was called. This was in the days when tea was most expensive and light beer was the common beverage in Europe, served even with meals in the upper class boarding schools. By my day, however, missionaries were expected to discourage drinking among the Inuit, and provincial laws banned it.

In the early 60s, at the request of the Inuit, the Newfoundland law against native drinking was rescinded on a trial basis. After more than twenty years the law is still on trial, and in that time alcohol has become a major problem in northern Labrador. The quiet, lovable, good-tempered Inuit become violent and cruel under the influence of alcohol, and liquor is involved in practically every criminal charge brought against them. Two of the chief reasons for this epidemic of alcoholism are the frustration of idleness at some seasons, and the indiscriminate access to liquor from local outlets.

Over the years, uninformed or unthinking critics have accused the Moravians of paternalism and over-protection of the Inuit, while in the same breath blaming change and the white man's influence for the excessive drinking. Missionaries have recognized the inevitability of change but also its dangers; in helping the Inuit to adapt slowly, to avoid being overwhelmed by change, they are charged with hindering progress.

Again there are some who accuse the missionaries of wielding great, even "unlimited" power over Inuit lives. Yet the missionaries' authority was only the power delegated to them by the *AngajoKauKattiget*. Undoubtedly some sought to exceed this power, but they were rarely successful. The Inuit and settler communities valued their rights and controlled their destinies more than most small communities in Newfoundland. More harm was done later when the Newfoundland government introduced its own municipal structure, undermining traditional self-government by setting up a rival form of local council.

Leaving Nain was not the end of my work. In Happy Valley I was entering a new phase, which entailed new responsibilities and new approaches to the problems of Labrador and its peoples. During the next fourteen years, spent among the settlers and Inuit of Happy Valley and North West River, my visits to the coast kept me in touch with life there. Yet I was now more able to travel to St. John's, to discuss problems with government officials.

During this period I made three memorable journeys. The first was to a conference of the World Council of Churches, in Montreal. Doris went with me, and we met many interesting and illustrious churchmen. The conference itself saddened us both, to see Christianity so divided in a world so much in need of healing, but it did lead to the formation of the Happy Valley Ministerial Association, our own local attempt at drawing the churches together.

The following year, in celebration of Jens Haven's first visit to Labrador in 1764, the Danish government and the Lutheran Church of Greenland and Denmark invited two Inuit and myself to Greenland on a fraternal visit. I was joined on this trip by my two old friends, Martin Martin and Natan Friede, both over seventy years old. The story of our adventures and of the wonderful hospitality we enjoyed must be told elsewhere, but I must say here that the visit was a joy and a success.

It was also clear from our visit that the problems of Greenland were eased by the fact that the Inuit formed a majority of the population, while the Inuit and Indians of Labrador are small minorities. Although alcohol was a problem in Greenland, too, it seemed less acute. I felt that our educational problems were about equal.

In 1967 Doris and I went to Czechoslovakia on the 500th anniversary of the Moravian Church, to attend a unity synod in the homeland of the *Unitas Fratrum*. Our visit lasted six weeks, and when we left we were grateful for the freedom and comfort Canadians enjoy. Wherever we went in that beautiful country we could sense an undercurrent of fear, and we felt deeply for our brethren in that communist society.

During my final fourteen years of service to the church, the years I spent in Happy Valley, I was honoured locally, provincially and nationally. Before we left Nain, in 1953, I had been awarded the Coronation Medal. In 1967 or 1968, the Happy Valley Chamber of Commerce recommended me for the Royal Bank of Canada award, given to an outstanding Canadian citizen. I lost out to Cardinal Leger, but counted myself honoured to have been a nominee. In 1969 I received the Order of Canada from Governor General Roland Michener, at an investiture at Government House. Two years later, I received an honorary degree of Doctor of Literature from Memorial University of Newfoundland. The same year a school in Happy Valley was named Peacock Academy in honour of Doris and me.

I felt that my colleagues and parishioners shared these honours, and especially that I owed my good fortune to the love, devotion, work and patience of my beloved wife, who has borne with my ills, my impatience and my idiosyncracies through forty-one years of marriage.

To have lived an exciting life, in work you enjoy, among people you love: what more can a man ask? Never did I regret going to Labrador, though sometimes I wondered why I was there. Nor do I now regret retiring to Newfoundland, which has accepted and adopted me as a son.

Now I wish to close by offering my deepest thanks to all the men and women, Inuit and white, who have contributed to a rewarding and happy life.

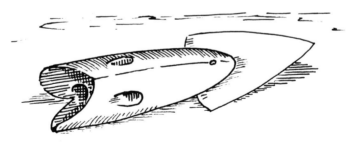

CENTURY OLD HARPOON HEAD

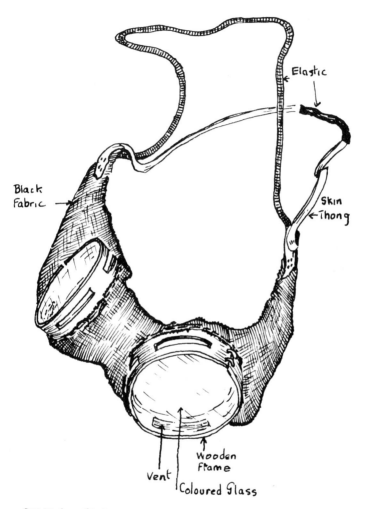

Elastic

Black
Fabric

Skin
Thong

Vent

Wooden
Frame

Coloured Glass

SNOW GLASSES

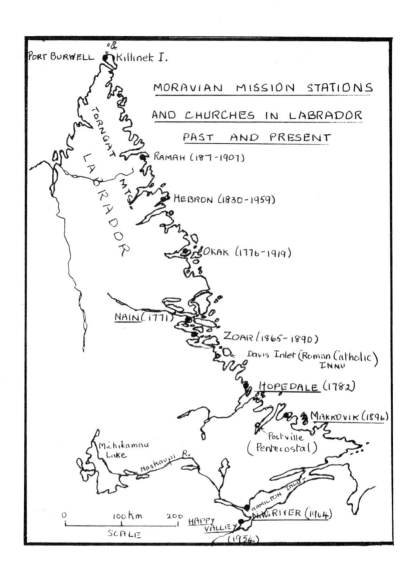

PORT BURWELL ● Killinek I.

MORAVIAN MISSION STATIONS

AND CHURCHES IN LABRADOR

PAST AND PRESENT

RAMAH (187-1907)

HEBRON (1830-1959)

OKAK (1776-1919)

NAIN (1771)

ZOAR (1865-1890)

Davis Inlet (Roman Catholic)
INNU

HOPEDALE (1782)

MAKKOVIK (1896)

Postville
(Pentecostal)

Michikamau Lake

Naskaupi R.

HAPPY VALLEY
(1954)

N.W. RIVER (1964)

0   100 Km   200
SCALE

TORNGAT MTS.

LABRADOR

HAMILTON INLET

PHOTOGRAPHS

Sculping dance performed by Simon of Hopedale
circa 1906—phase 1.

Sculping dance performed by Simon of Hopedale
circa 1906—phase 2.

Sculping dance performed by Simon of Hopedale
circa 1906—phase 3.

Sculping dance performed by Simon of Hopedale
circa 1906—phase 1.

Inuit sod houses circa 1906 at Hebron.

Church Mission House and out-buildings at Hopedale circa 1906.

Hebron Church and Mission House.

Hebron Church and Mission House —
sod houses in foreground

Firewood-cutting—Hebron

Bringing in brushwood for fuel—Hebron

Sod House

M. Holloway

Hebron Inuit woman

Hopedale Mission House and village—1906

Cirque, Middle Torngats

Tower Mountain looking east.

Middle Torngats

From Tower Mountain

Gulch Cape, Torngat Shore

Gordon Simmons

Torngat Mountains

Gordon Simmons

Cirque in Torngats

Gordon Simmons

Among the Torngats

Gordon Simmons

Tabular Iceberg— 200 ft. high, 1/2 mile in length